HOW TO WRITE A *DAMN* GOOD NOVEL, II

OTHER BOOKS BY JAMES N. FREY

NONFICTION

How to Write a Damn Good Novel

FICTION

Winter of the Wolves
Came a Dead Cat
Killing in Dreamland
The Long Way to Die
U.S.S.A.
The Last Patriot
The Armageddon Game
Circle of Death
The Elixir

HOW TO WRITE
A *DAMN* GOOD
NOVEL, II

ADVANCED
TECHNIQUES
FOR
DRAMATIC
STORYTELLING

JAMES N. FREY

St. Martin's Press • New York

Editor: George Witte
Production Editor: David Stanford Burr
Design: Judith A. Stagnitto

Library of Congress Cataloging-in-Publication Data

Frey, James N.
     How to write a damn good novel, II / James N.
Frey.
        p. cm.
    ISBN 0-312-10478-2
    1. Fiction—Technique.   I. Title.
PN 3365. F75   1994
808.3—dc20   93-44060
                         CIP

10 9 8 7 6

Books are available in quantity for promotional or premium
use. Write to Director of Special Sales, St. Martin's Press, 175
Fifth Avenue, New York, NY 10010, for information on dis-
counts and terms, or call toll-free (800) 221–7945. In New
York, call (212) 674–5151 (ext. 645).

IN MEMORIAM

Arnaldo Hernandez (1936–1993)
who lived and wrote passionately

ACKNOWLEDGMENTS

To my wife, Elizabeth, who suffers all the usual pains and uncertainties of being a writer's wife, and who labored long and hard copyediting the manuscript for this book; to Lester Gorn who taught me most of it; to Prof. Elizabeth Davis for her many great suggestions, enthusiasm, and occasional kick in the pants; to Susan Edmiston for her sharp-eyed editorial help; and to my agent, Susan Zeckendorf, without whom I might still be languishing as an insurance claims adjuster, spending my days calculating the cost of replacing dented bumpers.

CONTENTS

Introduction   1

CHAPTER ONE: The Fictive Dream and How to
Induce It   5
> To Dream Is Not to Sleep—Sympathy—
> Identification—Empathy—The Final Step: The
> Transported Reader

CHAPTER TWO: All About Suspense or Pass the
Mustard, I'm Biting My Nails   21
> Suspense Defined—Lighting the Fuse

CHAPTER THREE: Of Wimps and Wackos: Creating
Truly Memorable Characters   33
> Wimps—Characters Worth Knowing—Character
> and Competence—The Wacky Factor—Character
> Contrast and Setting—The Ruling Passions—Dual
> Characters

CHAPTER FOUR: The "P" Word (Premise)
Revisited: Part One: The Concept Is Explained and
Simplified   49
> A Rose by Any Other Name Is Not a Banana—
> Finding a Premise for a Particular Story—Sorting

Out the Babble of Terms—Premises at Work—A
Mighty Example—Types of Premises

CHAPTER FIVE: The "P" Word (Premise) Revisited:
Part Two: The Novelist's Magic Wand   63
    Premise Prestidigitation—Premise-Making for Fun
    and Profit—The Multipremise Novel—Mastering
    the Technique of Writing with a Premise

CHAPTER SIX: On Voice or The "Who" Who Tells
the Tale   79
    Why the Who Ain't You—The Roar of the Lion:
    Using a Strong Narrative Voice—The First versus
    Third Pseudo-Rule and Other Myths—The Writer
    Pumping Iron: Developing Your Voice

CHAPTER SEVEN: The Author/Reader Contract or
Don't Promise a Primrose and Deliver a Pickle   99
    The Basic Contract—Genre—Mainstream—
    Literary—The Contract beyond the Conventions—
    The Unreliable Narrator—Playing Fair

CHAPTER EIGHT: The Seven Deadly Mistakes   111
    1. Timidity—2. Trying to Be Literary—3. Ego-
    Writing—4. Failure to Learn to Re-dream the
    Dream—5. Failure to Keep Faith with Yourself—
    6. Wrong Lifestyle—7. Failure to Produce

CHAPTER NINE: Writing with Passion   137
    Why Now Is the Best Time in History to Be a
    Fiction Writer—The James N. Frey 100 Percent
    Guarantee of Success—Creating a Masterpiece

Tell them to write as honestly as they can. Tell them to ponder their characters to make sure that the emotions their characters feel and the decisions their characters make—their choices, their courses of action—are consistent with the characters they have envisioned. And tell them to check and recheck each sentence to be sure they have communicated what they intended to communicate. And to ask themselves, What does this sentence say? Are its nuances the nuances I want? Tell them that's what they have to do if they aspire to write a damn good novel.

—LESTER GORN

HOW TO WRITE A *DAMN* GOOD NOVEL, II

INTRODUCTION

There are a scores of books for the beginning fiction writer on the bookstore shelf, most of them helpful. A few of them, such as Lajos Egri's *The Art of Dramatic Writing* (1946), Jack M. Bickman's *Writing Novels That Sell* (1989), Raymond C. Knott's *The Craft of Fiction* (1977), Jean Z. Owen's *Professional Fiction Writing* (1974), and William Foster-Harris's mighty little masterpiece, *The Basic Formulas of Fiction* (1944), are extraordinary.

And then, of course, there's James N. Frey's *How to Write a Damn Good Novel* (1987), which modesty prevents me from recommending, even though it's gone through several printings and is widely used as a text in novel-writing workshops in this country and has been reprinted in England and in Europe and was recommended by *Writer's Digest* even though they didn't publish it, and . . .

Never mind that.

The point is, there are some damn good books that cover the fundamentals of fiction writing and explain things like how to create dynamic characters, the nature and purpose of conflict, how characters develop, finding a premise and how it's used, how conflicts rise to a climax and resolution, point of view, the use of sensuous and colorful language, the writing of good, snappy dialogue, and so on.

But this book is different.

This book was written with the assumption that the reader is already familiar with the basics and hungers to know more. This book covers advanced techniques such as how to make your characters not just dynamic but memorable, how to heighten the reader's sympathy and identification with the characters, how to intensify suspense to keep the reader gripped, how to make a contract with the reader and stick to it, how to avoid the fiction writer's seven deadly mistakes, and perhaps most important of all, how to write with passion.

There's another way in which this book differs from books for beginners: it does not lay down pseudo-rules as holy writ. Most books on fictional techniques are written by creative-writing teachers who find, for example, that their beginning students can't control viewpoint, so they make a pseudo-rule that "you can't change viewpoint within the scene," or that their students are often too pontifical or didactic in their work, so they make a rule that "the author must remain invisible." Fledgling authors who can't make the narrative voice fit their fictional material are often told, "First-person narrative is more restrictive than third-person, but it's more intimate, so if you want greater intimacy you better stick with first."

Such admonitions and pseudo-rules are total bunkum and following such rules is like trying to be an Olympic swimmer with an anchor tied to your foot.

Actually, pseudo-rules are taught to beginners to make life easier for the creative-writing teacher. The pseudo-rules help beginning authors *appear* to be in control of their material. I was taught a host of pseudo-rules by some of the very finest creative-writing teachers in America; I believed in the pseudo-rules fervently, and in turn, years later, inflicted them on my students. Now, I realize there's a difference between pseudo-rules and effective principles: pseudo-rules are coffins; effective principles are cannons into which you stuff the gunpowder of your talent.

In this book, many pseudo-rules will be vaporized. You'll read, as an example, how viewpoints *can* be switched effectively within a scene, how the author *can* intervene almost at will (depending on the contract that's been made with the reader), and how you *can* achieve total intimacy no matter which viewpoint you choose.

We'll also discuss further the uses and abuses of the concept of premise, how to make the reader dream the fictive dream, how to create more complex and memorable characters, and how to write with the formal genres, as defined by the New York publishing industry, in mind.

Before we begin, please understand this book is not for everyone, even if you are *not* a beginner.

As was the case in *How to Write a Damn Good Novel*, the principles of novel writing under discussion apply to works to be written in the dramatic form. If you aspire to write another kind of novel—experimental, modernist, postmodernist, minimalist, symbolic, philosophical, a memoir, metafiction, or any other kind not cast in the dramatic form—this book is not for you.

But if what you want to write is a gripping, emotionally charged, dramatic novel—and you already have a command of the basic principles of fiction writing—then please, come join the feast.

ONE

THE FICTIVE DREAM AND HOW TO INDUCE IT

TO DREAM IS NOT TO SLEEP

If you're going to succeed in a service business, you've got to know why people come to you for services and what you can do to satisfy them.

If you run a janitorial business, say, you've got to know that people like shiny floors and sparkling porcelain. If you're a divorce lawyer, you've got to know your client not only wants a big settlement and alimony, but also wants his or her ex to suffer. Fiction writing is a service business. Before you sit down to write a damn good novel, you ought to know what your readers want.

If you were writing nonfiction, what your readers want would depend on the kind of book you're writing. A self-help book on how to get rich will have chapters on keeping faith in yourself, sticking to it, stroking the IRS, and so on. A sex manual should have lots of pictures and make exaggerated claims about the spiritual growth of the practitioners of the prescribed contortions. A biography of Sir Wilbur Mugaby should deliver all the scandalous facts of the old reprobate's life. If you were going to write a nonfiction book, you would concern yourself mainly with *informing* the reader. A nonfiction writer makes arguments and relates facts.

A fiction writer isn't arguing anything, and what the fiction writer is relating is hardly fact. There's little knowledge, in the ordinary sense, to be gained. It's all made-up stuff, totally fraudulent,

5

a rendering of events that never happened concerning people who never were. Why would anyone with half a brain in his or her melon buy this pap?

Some of the reasons are obvious. A mystery reader expects to be baffled in the beginning and dazzled with the detective's brilliance in the end. In a historical novel, say, the reader expects to get a taste for the way things were in the good old days. In a romance, the reader expects a plucky heroine, a handsome hero, and a lot of steamy passion.

Bernard DeVoto in *The World of Fiction* (1956) says people read for "pleasure . . . professional and semi-professional people aside, no one ever reads fiction for aught else." And it's true, people do read for pleasure, but there's far more to it than that. As a fiction writer, you're expected to *transport* a reader. Readers are said to be transported when, while they are reading, they feel that they are actually living in the story world and the real world around them evaporates.

A transported reader is dreaming the *fictive dream*. "This," says John Gardner in *The Art of Fiction* (1984), "no matter the genre, [the fictive dream] is the way fiction does its work."

The fictive dream is created by the power of suggestion. The power of suggestion is the operant tool of the ad man, the con man, the propagandist, the priest, the hypnotist, and, yes, the fiction writer. The ad man, the con man, the propagandist, and the priest use the power of suggestion to persuade. Both the hypnotist and the fiction writer use it to invoke a state of altered consciousness.

Wow, you say, sounds mystical almost. And in a way it is.

When the power of suggestion is used by the hypnotist, the result is a trance. A hypnotist sits you in a chair and you look at a shiny object, say a pendant. The hypnotist gently swings the pendant and intones: "Your eyelids are getting heavy, you feel yourself getting more and more relaxed, more and more relaxed, as you listen to the sound of my voice. . . . As your eyes begin to close you find yourself on a stairway in your mind, going down, down, down to where it's dark and quiet, dark and quiet . . . " And, amazingly, you find yourself feeling more and more relaxed.

The hypnotist continues: "You find yourself on a path in a beautiful garden. It is quiet and peaceful here. It's a lazy summer's day, the sun is out, there's a warm breeze blowing, the magnolias are in bloom . . . "

As the hypnotist says these words, the objects that the hypnotist mentions—the garden, the path, the magnolias—appear on the viewing screen of your mind. You will experience the breeze, the sun, the smell of the flowers. You are now in a trance.

The fiction writer uses identical devices to bring the reader into the fictive dream. The fiction writer offers specific images that create a scene on the viewing screen of the reader's mind. In hypnosis, the protagonist of the little story the hypnotist tells is "you," meaning the subject. The fiction writer may use "you," but the more usual practice is to use "I" or "he" or "she." The effect is the same.

Most books on fiction writing advise the writer to "show, not tell." An example of "telling" is this: "He walked into the garden and found it very beautiful." The writer is *telling* how it was, not *showing* how it was. An example of "showing" is this: "He walked into the silent garden at sundown and felt the soft breeze blowing through the holly bushes and found the scent of jasmine strong in the air."

As John Gardner, again in *The Art of Fiction,* says, "vivid detail is the life blood of fiction . . . the reader is regularly presented with proofs—in the form of closely observed details . . . it's physical detail that pulls us into a story, makes us believe." When a writer is "showing," he or she is suggesting the sensuous detail that draws the reader into the fictive dream. "Telling" pushes the reader out of the fictive dream, because it requires the reader to make a conscious analysis of what's being told, which brings the reader into a waking state. It forces the reader to think, not feel.

The reading of fiction, then, is the experience of a dream working at the subconscious level. This is the reason most sensible people hate the academic study of literature. Academics attempt to make rational and logical something that is intended to make you dream. Reading *Moby Dick* and analyzing the imagery is to read it in a waking state. The author wants you to be absorbed into the story world, to go on a voyage on the *Pequod* halfway around the globe in search of a whale, not to be bogged down figuring how he did it, or to be looking for the hidden meaning of the symbolism as if it were a game of hide-and-seek played by the author and the reader.

Once the writer has created a word picture for the reader, the next step is to get the reader involved emotionally. This is done by gaining the reader's sympathy.

7

Sympathy is often given little more than a passing nod by the authors of how-to-write-fiction books. Gaining the reader's sympathy for your characters is crucial to inducing the fictive dream, and if you don't effectively induce the fictive dream, you haven't written a damn good novel.

Sympathy is a frequently misunderstood concept. Some how-to-write-fiction authors have made a pseudo-rule that says that for a reader to have sympathy for a character, the character must be *admirable*. This is patently *not* true. Most readers have a lot of sympathy for a character like, say, Defoe's Moll Flanders, or Dickens's Fagin in *Oliver Twist,* or Long John Silver in Stevenson's *Treasure Island.* Yet these characters are not admirable in the least. Moll Flanders is a liar, a thief, and a bigamist; Fagin corrupts youth; and Long John Silver is a rascal, a cheat, and a pirate.

A few years ago there was a film called *Raging Bull* about former middleweight boxing champion Jake LaMotta. The character in the film beat his wife, then divorced her when he started to succeed in the ring. He seduced girls who were not of legal age, had a violent temper fueled by paranoia, and spoke in grunts. He was a total savage in the ring and on the street. Yet the character of LaMotta, played by Robert De Niro in the film, garnered a great deal of audience sympathy.

How was this miracle accomplished?

Jake LaMotta at the start of the film was living in ignorance, degradation, and poverty, and the audience *felt sorry* for him. This is the key: To gain the sympathy of your reader, make the reader feel sorry for the character. In Victor Hugo's *Les Misérables,* as an example, Jean Valjean is introduced to the reader as he arrives wearily at a town and goes to the inn to eat. Although he has money, he is refused service. He is starving. The reader must feel sorry for this hapless man, no matter what dreadful crime he may have committed.

- In *Jaws* (1974), Peter Benchley introduces his protagonist Brody at the moment he gets the call to go out and look for a girl missing in the sea. Already aware that the girl is the victim of a shark attack, the reader knows what Brody is about to face. The reader will feel sorry for him.

• In *Carrie* (1974), Stephen King introduces Carrie in this manner: "Girls stretched and writhed under the hot water, squalling, flicking water, squirting white bars of soap from hand to hand. Carrie stood among them stolidly, a frog among swans." King describes her as fat, pimply, and so on. She's ugly and picked on. Readers feel sorry for Carrie.

• In *Pride and Prejudice* (1813), Jane Austen introduces us to her heroine, Elizabeth Bennet, at a dance, where Mr. Bingley tries to induce his friend, Mr. Darcy, to dance with her. Darcy says: " 'Which do you mean?' and turning round he looked for a moment at Elizabeth, till catching her eye, he withdrew his own and coldly said, 'She is tolerable, but not handsome enough to tempt me . . . ' " Obviously, the reader feels sorry for Elizabeth in her humiliation.

• In *Crime and Punishment* (1872), Dostoevsky introduces Raskolnikov in a state of "morbid terror" because he owes his landlady money and has fallen into a state of "nervous depression." The reader is compelled to feel sorry for a man in a state of such dire poverty.

• In *The Trial* (1937), Kafka introduces us to Joseph K. at the moment he is arrested, compelling the reader to feel sorry for poor K.

• In *The Red Badge of Courage* (1895), we meet Henry, the protagonist, as a "youthful private" who's in an army about to go on the attack. He's terrified. The reader, again, will feel sorry for him.

• The very first thing we're told about Scarlett O'Hara in *Gone with the Wind* (1936) is that she is not beautiful and she's trying to get a beau. In matters of amour, the reader always feels sorry for those who haven't found it.

Certain other situations will also automatically guarantee winning the reader's sympathy. Situations of loneliness, lovelessness, humiliation, privation, repression, embarrassment, danger—virtually any predicament that brings physical, mental, or spiritual suffering to the character—will earn the reader's sympathy.

Sympathy is the doorway through which the reader gains emotional access to a story. Without sympathy, the reader has no emotional involvement in the story. Having gained sympathy, bring the reader further into the fictive dream by getting him or her to identify with the character.

IDENTIFICATION

Identification is often confused with sympathy. Sympathy is achieved when a reader feels sorry for the character's plight. But a reader might feel sorry for a loathsome wretch who is about to be hung without identifying with him. Identification occurs when the reader is not only in sympathy with the character's plight, but also supports his or her goals and aspirations and has a strong desire that the character achieve them.

- In *Jaws,* the reader supports Brody's goal to destroy the shark.

- In *Carrie,* the reader supports Carrie's longings to go to the prom against her tyrannical mother's wishes.

- In *Pride and Prejudice,* the reader supports Elizabeth's desire to fall in love and get married.

- In *The Trial,* the reader supports K.'s determination to free himself from the clutches of the law.

- In *Crime and Punishment,* the reader supports Raskolnikov's need to escape from poverty.

- In *The Red Badge of Courage,* the reader supports Henry's desire to prove to himself he is no coward.

- In *Gone with the Wind,* the reader supports Scarlett's craving to get her plantation back after it is destroyed by Yankees.

Fine, you say, but what if you're writing about a loathsome wretch? How do you get the reader to identify then? Easy.

Say you have a character who's in prison. He's treated horribly, beaten by the guards, beaten by the other prisoners, abandoned by his family. Even though he may be guilty as Cain, the reader will feel sorry for him, so you've won the reader's sympathy. But will the reader identify with him?

Say his goal is to bust out of prison. The reader will not *necessarily* identify with his goal because he's, say, a vicious killer. A reader who wants him to stay in prison will identify with the prosecutors, judges, juries, and guards, who want him kept right where he is. It is possible, though, for the reader to identify with the prisoner's goal if he has a desire to reform and make amends for what he's done. Give your character a goal that is noble, and the reader will take his side, no matter how much of a degenerate slime he has proven himself to be in the past.

Mario Puzo had a problem when he wrote *The Godfather*. His protagonist, Don Corleone, made a living by loan-sharking, running protection rackets, and corrupting labor unions. Hardly someone you'd want to invite over for an evening of pinochle. To stay in business, Don Corleone bribed politicians, bought newsmen, bullied Italian shopkeepers into selling only *Genco Pura* olive oil, and made offers impossible to refuse. Let's face it, Don Corleone was a degenerate slime of the first rank. Not a character a reader would be likely to sympathize and identify with. Yet Puzo wanted readers to sympathize and identify with Don Corleone and he was able to get them to do it. Millions of people who read the book and millions more who saw the film did sympathize and identify with Don Corleone. How did Mario Puzo work this miracle? He did it with a stroke of genius, creating the magic of sympathy for a character who had suffered an injustice and linking Don Corleone with a noble goal.

Mario Puzo did not begin his story with Don Corleone fitting out some poor slob with a pair of cement shoes, which would have caused the reader to despise him. Instead, he begins with a hardworking undertaker, Amerigo Bonasera, standing in an American courtroom as he "waited for justice; vengeance on the men who had so cruelly hurt his daughter, who had tried to dishonor her." But the judge lets the boys get off with a suspended sentence. As Puzo's narrator tells us:

> All his years in America, Amerigo Bonasera had trusted in law and order. And he had prospered thereby. Now, though his brain smoked with hatred, though wild visions of buying a gun and killing the two young men

jangled the very bones of his skull, Bonasera turned to his still uncomprehending wife and explained to her, "They have made fools of us." He paused and then made his decision, no longer fearing the cost. "For justice we must go on our knees to Don Corleone."

Obviously, the reader is in sympathy with Mr. Bonasera, who wants only justice for his daughter. And since Mr. Bonasera must go to Don Corleone to get justice, our sympathy is transferred to Don Corleone, the man who brings justice. Puzo forges a positive emotional bond between the reader and Don Corleone through sympathy, by creating a situation where the reader identifies with Don Corleone's goal of obtaining justice for poor Mr. Bonasera and his unfortunate daughter.

Next, Puzo reinforces the reader's identification with Don Corleone when he has "the Turk" approach him to deal dope and the Don—as a matter of high principle—refuses; the reader identifies with Don Corleone even more. By giving the Don a code of personal honor, Puzo helps the reader to dismiss his or her revulsion for crime bosses. Instead of loathing Don Corleone, the reader is fully in sympathy with him, identifying with him and championing his cause.

EMPATHY

Despite feeling sorry for a character who is experiencing, say, loneliness, the reader may not feel the loneliness itself. But through empathy with the character, the reader will feel what the character is feeling. Empathy is a much more powerful emotion than sympathy.

Sometimes when a wife goes into labor a husband will also suffer labor pains. This is an example of empathy. The husband is not just in sympathy; he empathizes to the point of suffering actual, physical pain.

Say you go to a funeral. You don't know the deceased, Herman Weatherby; he was a brother of your friend Agnes. Your friend is grieving, but you're not. You didn't even know Herman. You feel sorry for Agnes because she's so sad.

The funeral service has not started yet. You and Agnes go for a walk in the churchyard. She starts to tell you what her brother Herman was like. He was studying to be a physical therapist so that he could devote his life to helping crippled kids walk. He had a wonderful sense of humor, he did a great Richard Nixon imitation at parties, and once in college he threw a pie in the face of a professor who gave him a *D*. Sounds like Herman was a fun guy.

As Agnes brings her brother back to life so you can get to know him, you begin to feel something beyond mere sympathy. You begin to sense the loss to the world of this intelligent, creative, wacky man—you are beginning to empathize with your friend, and now you begin to feel the grief your friend is feeling. Such is the power of empathy.

Now then, how does a fiction writer get the reader to empathize?

Say you're writing a story about Sam Smoot, a dentist. Sam's a gambler. He loses $2 million to a mobster and is ruined, and his family is ruined as well. How do you get the reader to empathize? The reader may feel sorry for his family, but may also feel that Sam got what was coming to him.

Even so, you can gain empathy.

You do it by using the power of suggestion. You use sensuous and emotion-provoking details that suggest to the reader what it is like to be Sam and to suffer what he is suffering. In other words, you create the story world in such a way that readers can put themselves in the character's place:

> A cold wind gusted down Main Street and the wet snow had already started to fall. Sam's toes felt numb in his shoes, and the hunger in his belly had started gnawing at him again. His nose was running. He wiped it on his sleeve, no longer caring how it looked.

By using sensuous and emotion-provoking detail, you bring the reader inside Sam's world to experience what Sam is experiencing. You can win empathy for a character by detailing the sensuous details in the environment: the sights, sounds, pains, smells, and so on that the character is feeling—the feelings that trigger his emotions:

> Sam woke up on the third day and looked around.
> The room had white walls and there were white curtains

over the window. A large-screen TV was mounted high on the wall. The sheets smelled clean, and there were flowers on the table next to the bed. He felt his body. It was hard to tell it was there because it wasn't cold and it wasn't hurting. Not even his belly, which had been hurting now for so long . . .

Such emotion-provoking sensuous details, through the power of suggestion, will evoke the reader's emotions and propitiate the reader's empathy.

Here's an example of emotion-provoking sensuous detail from Stephen King's *Carrie:*

> She [Carrie] put the dress on for the first time on the morning of May 27, in her room. She had bought a special brassiere to go with it, which gave her breasts the proper uplift. . . . Wearing it gave her a weird, dreamy feeling that was half shame and half defiant excitement.

Notice how the detail (the brassiere, the proper uplift) and the emotion (a weird, dreamy feeling, half shame, half excitement) are tied together. A few paragraphs later, Carrie's uptight mother opens the door:

> They looked at each other.
> Hardly conscious of it, Carrie felt her back straighten until she stood straight in the patch of early spring sunshine that fell through the window.

The back straightening is symbolic defiance, a powerful emotion tied to the sensuous detail of standing in the patch of light.

Sympathizing with Carrie because her mother is persecuting her, the reader identifies with her goal to go to the prom, and empathizes with her because the author creates the reality with emotion-provoking sensuous details.

In *The Red Badge of Courage* Stephen Crane strives to evoke empathy by using the same kind of emotion-provoking sensuous details this way:

One gray dawn, however, he was kicked in the leg by the tall soldier, and then, before he was entirely awake, he found himself running down a wooded road in the midst of men who were panting from the first effects of speed. His canteen banged rhythmically upon his thigh and his haversack bobbed softly. His musket bounced a trifle from his shoulder at each stride and made his cap feel uncertain upon his head.... The youth thought the damp fog of early morning moved from the rush of a great body of troops. From the distance came a sudden spatter of firing.

He was bewildered. As he ran with his comrades he strenuously tried to think, but all he knew was that if he fell down those coming behind would tread upon him. All his faculties seemed to be needed to guide him over and past obstructions. He felt carried away by a mob.... The youth felt like the time had come. He was about to be measured ...

Notice the details that connect with his senses: the dampness of the fog, the banging of the canteen against his thigh, the bobbing of the haversack, the bouncing of his rifle, the cap uncertain upon his head. Crane carefully constructs the reality of war out of small details leading to the youth's feelings that he's being "carried away by a mob" and is "about to measured." The reader is in sympathy with the hero (and would feel sorry for any man about to face possible death in combat), identifies with his goal (to find his courage and prove himself a man), and empathizes with him because the reality of the situation is created through emotion-provoking sensuous detail.

Here's an example from *Jaws:*

Brody sat in the swiveled fighting chair bolted to the deck, trying to stay awake. He was hot and sticky. There had been no breeze at all during the six hours they had been sitting and waiting. The back of his neck was already badly sunburned, and every time he moved his head the collar of his uniform shirt raked the tender skin. His body odor rose to his face and, blended with the stench of the fish guts and blood being ladled overboard, nauseated him. He felt poached.

The reader is put squarely in that chair, feeling the chafe of the collar, the heat of the sun, the nausea. Brody is in an unpleasant holding pattern, waiting for the shark.

Kafka has K. in a similar situation, waiting for his trial:

> One winter morning—snow was falling outside the window in a foggy dimness—K. was sitting in his office, already exhausted in spite of the early hour. To save his face before his subordinates at least, he had given his clerk instructions to admit no one, on the plea that he was occupied with an important piece of work. But instead of working he twisted in his chair, idly rearranged the things lying on his writing table, and then, without being aware of it, let his outstretched arm rest on the table and went on sitting motionless with bowed head.

Again, it's the details: the foggy dimness, twisting in his chair, letting his outstretched arm rest on the table, and so on.

Sympathy, identification, and empathy all help to create an emotional bond between the reader and the characters. At this point you are on the brink of transporting your reader.

THE FINAL STEP: THE TRANSPORTED READER

When transported, the reader goes into a sort of bubble, utterly involved in the fictional world to the point that the real world evaporates. This is the aim of the fiction writer: to bring the reader to the point of complete absorption with the characters and their world.

In hypnosis, this is called the *plenary state*. The hypnotist, in control, suggests that the subject quack like a duck, and the subject happily complies. If a fiction writer gets the reader into the plenary state, the reader weeps, laughs, and feels the pain of the character, thinks the character's thoughts, and participates in the character's decisions.

Readers in this state can be so absorbed they have to be distracted, often physically shaken, to get their attention. "Hey, Charlie! Put that book down! Dinner's ready! Hey! You deaf?"

So how do you get the reader from sympathy, identification, and empathy to being totally absorbed? The answer: inner conflict.

Inner conflict is the storm raging inside the characters: doubts, misgivings, guilts, remorse, indecision. Once in sympathy, identification, and empathy with the characters, the reader will be open to suffer their pangs of remorse, feel their guilt, experience their doubts and misgivings, and, most important of all, take sides in the decisions they are forced to make. These decisions are almost always of a moral nature and have grave consequences for the character. His or her honor or self-worth will be at stake.

It is this participation in the decision-making process, when the reader is feeling the character's guilt, doubts, misgivings, and remorse, and is pulling for the character to make one decision over another, that transports the reader. Here's an example from *Carrie*. In this scene, Carrie is awaiting her date for the prom, not knowing whether he will come:

> She opened her eyes again. The Black Forest cuckoo clock, bought with Green Stamps, said seven-ten.
> (he'll be here in twenty minutes)
> Would he?
> Maybe it was all just an elaborate joke, the final crusher, the ultimate punch line. To leave her sitting here half the night in her crushed-velvet prom gown with its princess waistline, juliet sleeves and simple straight skirt—and her tea roses pinned to her left shoulder . . . Carrie did not think anyone could understand the brute courage it had taken to reconcile herself to this, to leave herself open to whatever fearsome possibilities the night might realize. Being stood up could hardly be the worst of them. In fact, in a kind of sneaking, wishful way she thought it might be for the best if—
> (no stop that)
> Of course it would be easier to stay here with Momma. Safer. She knew what They thought of Mom-

ma. Well maybe Momma was a fanatic, a freak, but at least she was predictable . . .

Notice how, when the character is in the throes of an inner conflict, there's an equal pull in two directions. Carrie desperately wants to go to the prom, yet it's so much safer to stay home.

Franz Kafka puts Joseph K. in the throes of an inner conflict like this:

> K. paused and stared at the ground before him. For the moment he was still free, he could continue on his way and vanish through one of the small, dark, wooden doors that faced him at no great distance. It would simply indicate that he had not understood the call, or that he had understood it and did not care. But if he were to turn round he would be caught, for that would amount to an admission that he had understood it very well, that he really was the person addressed, and that he was ready to obey . . .

It is a small decision, but one with possibly grave consequences. Should he go through the door or not? The reader, too, will share the dilemma.

Stephen Crane puts his hero through inner conflict like this:

> This advance upon Nature was too calm. He had opportunity to reflect. He had time in which to wonder about himself and to attempt to probe his sensations.
>
> Absurd ideas took hold of him. He thought that he did not relish the landscape. It threatened him. A coldness swept over his back, and it is true that his trousers felt to him that they were not fit for his legs at all.
>
> A house standing placidly in distant fields had to him an ominous look. The shadows of the woods were formidable. He was certain that in this vista there lurked fierce-eyed hosts. The swift thought came to him that the generals did not know what they were about. It was all a trap. Suddenly those close forests would bristle with rifle barrels. Ironlike brigades would appear in the rear. They were all going to be sacrificed. The generals were

18

stupid. The enemy would presently swallow the whole command. He glared about him, expecting to see the stealthy approach of his death.

He thought that he must break from the ranks and harangue his comrades. They must not all be killed like pigs; and he was sure it would come to pass unless they were informed of these dangers. The generals were idiots to send them marching into a regular pen. There was but one pair of eyes in the corps. He would step forth to make a speech. Shrill and passionate words came to his lips . . . as he looked the youth gripped his outcry at his throat. He saw that even if the men were tottering with fear they would laugh at his warning. They would jeer him, and, if practicable, pelt him with missiles. Admitting that he might be wrong, a frenzied declamation of the kind would turn him into a worm.

Henry is in the throes of an inner conflict that is tearing him apart. His terror is getting the best of him, and soon he will resolve this inner conflict by running away in the face of the enemy.

In *Crime and Punishment*, Dostoevsky puts his hero in the throes of an intense inner conflict as he contemplates murder:

Raskolnikov made his exit in a perturbed state of mind. As he went downstairs, he stopped from time to time, as if overcome by violent emotion. When he had at length emerged upon the street, he exclaimed to himself: "How loathsome it all is! Can I, can I ever?—no, it's absurd, preposterous! How could such a horrible idea ever enter my head? Could I ever be capable of such infamy? It is odious, ignoble, repulsive! And yet for a whole month—"

The loathing sense of disgust which had begun to oppress him on his way to the old woman's house had now become so intense that he longed to find some way of escape from the torture . . .

Dostoevsky is a master of inner conflict. Here, it has occurred to Raskolnikov that the solution to his problems of poverty is to commit a murder, yet his conscience is having a volcanic eruption. Dostoevsky's genius lay in his ability to put his characters into an intense inner conflict and keep them there for most of the story, thereby keeping the reader totally transported.

Inner conflict can be thought of as a battle between two "voices" within the character: one of reason, the other of passion— or of two conflicting passions. One, a protagonist, the other, an antagonist (Agnes thought: I'm gonna kill him when he gets home, flatten his damn skull! But what if he's in one of his sweet moods? What if he's singing that love song he wrote for me? No matter! The minute he walks through that door he's a dead man!). These voices are in a rising conflict that usually comes to some kind of climax, where a decision is made that leads to an action. When you think of characters in the throes of inner conflict, think of them as having two competing, equally desirable choices of action, each supported by its own voice. The character then is on the horns of a dilemma, and that's just where you want him or her to be.

To keep your reader transported, dreaming the fictive dream deeply, it's a good idea to heighten suspense, which, happily, is the subject of Chapter Two.

TWO

ALL ABOUT·SUSPENSE OR PASS THE MUSTARD, I'M BITING MY NAILS

SUSPENSE DEFINED

William Foster-Harris, in *The Basic Formulas of Fiction*, says "we do our best to paralyze the reader—freeze him to the book. All quivering helplessness, he waits to see what is going to happen next." Freezing the quivering and helpless reader to the book is what a novelist lives for. To do that, the novelist tries to make his or her readers "worry and wonder" about characters. "Worrying and wondering" is another way of saying the reader is being held in suspense.

Webster's defines suspense this way:

Suspense: n, 1. The state of being undecided or undetermined.

What is it that is undecided or undetermined? It is not the author, certainly. And not the reader, either. What is undecided or undetermined is a *story question.*

A story question is a device to make the reader curious. Story questions are usually not put in question form. They are rather statements that require further explanation, problems that require resolution, forecasts of crisis, and the like.

Here are a few examples of story openings that raise story questions:

- It was well after midnight when the rector heard a loud banging on the door. (The question: Who might be knocking so late at night, and why?)

- The first thing Harriet said to herself when she met George was, "Father will never, ever approve of this man." (Questions raised: Will George like Harriet? Why won't her father approve? What will happen when George and the father meet? Is Harriet interested in George, or does she just like to needle her father?)

- Linus met his new stepmother for the first time on Christmas Eve. (Question raised: Will they like each other?)

- Henry didn't believe in ghosts. (Question: Will this disbelief be put to the test?)

- When her husband called at four o'clock and said he was bringing the boss to dinner, Lydia was in the middle of doing a valve job on their '56 Buick. (Question: How will she bring the dinner off?)

- His Ma told Jeb not to strap the old Colt on his hip when he went into Tombstone, but Jeb never did listen to nobody. (Question: What dire thing will happen when he brings this gun to town?)

- "Oh!" Jenny exclaimed, "you brought me a gift!" (Question: What's the gift?)

Raising story questions of this type is the simplest and most direct way to create suspense.

Story questions, unless they are powerful, life-and-death questions that are strengthened, reinforced, and elaborated, will not hold the reader long. When they appear in the beginning of a story, they are called *hooks* because they are intended to "hook" the reader into reading more.

Hooks are often short-range story questions that will be answered in the story quickly, but they could be long-range story questions that will not be answered until nearly the end of the story.

Remember the old western movies where the hero was given until sundown to fulfill a mission? The viewer had to wait until the end of the movie to see whether he would succeed.

A story question, sometimes called a tease, is an attention-grabbing device. It arouses readers' curiosity, getting them interested in the story. But the technique of raising story questions can be mishandled. Macauley and Lanning in *Technique in Fiction* (1987) warn that "a writer has to discriminate wisely between the attention-getting device that soon becomes fairly irrelevant to the story and the beginning that genuinely gathers the reader into the arms of the story . . . an exciting, dramatic beginning is entirely possible, but it must be justified completely by the story that follows." In other words, play fair with your reader. Be sure your story questions raise legitimate questions about the characters and their situation.

Beginning writers will often start a story without raising a story question. What follow are a few examples of the kinds of opening lines often written by beginners:

- Ginger's bedroom had striped wallpaper on the walls and a desk under the window. (Questions raised: none.)

- Ocean City was no place to have fun at night, so Oswald decided to go to bed early and read about how to make a paper airplane. (This is a sort of negative story question; the reader doesn't want to read on because he doesn't want to be bored.)

- The old Ford had a rusted paint job and a horsehair seat that smelled like an old pair of sneakers. (Again, no question being raised—description only.)

- Her teacher had been a witch, and Maggie was glad when summer vacation came. (The problem that arises out of having a teacher who's a witch is about to resolve itself. There's no question raised in the reader's mind about what's going to happen next.)

- The warm sea breeze blew in through the open window, and the moon overhead was a golden globe on the horizon of the Santa Cruz Mountains. (Sounds like a fiction story all right, but it isn't going to hook a reader.)

Such openings often doom a story, even a good one, because editors and readers will not stay with a story long if their interest has not been piqued.

Here's an example from a published novel, where story questions are being raised:

> An hour before sunset, on the evening of a day in the beginning of October, 1815, a man travelling afoot entered the little town of D——. The few persons who at this time were at their windows or their doors, regarded this traveller with a sort of distrust.

This is the opening of the second book of Victor Hugo's *Les Misérables*. The first sentence raises the story question, Who is this man? The second sentence modifies it to make him slightly ominous, which increases the suspense. The reader's curiosity has certainly been piqued.

Most books that purport to give advice to fiction writers will claim that it is wise for writers of short stories to hook their readers as soon as possible, in the first three paragraphs or so, but the novelist, it's often claimed, has more space. Here is yet another bunkum pseudo-rule. Both the short-story writer and the novelist should present a story question as soon as possible, usually in the first or second sentence.

Here are some examples:

• The great fish moved silently through the night water, propelled by short sweeps of its crescent tail. (From *Jaws*, of course. The story question raised: Who will be the shark's lunch?)

• Someone must have traduced Joseph K., for without having done anything wrong, he was arrested one fine morning. (*The Trial*. This opening sentence raises all kinds of story questions. Why was he arrested? What will happen to him? Who turned him in and why?)

• It is a truth universally acknowledged, that a single man in possession of a good fortune must be in want of a wife. (*Pride and Prejudice*. This raises the obvious story questions: Who's the single man? And who's going to be the lucky girl?)

• The cold passed reluctantly from the earth, and the retiring fogs revealed an army stretched out on the hills, resting. As the landscape changed from brown to green, the army awakened, and began to tremble with eagerness at the noise of rumors. (*The Red Badge of Courage.* The question here: What are the rumors?)

• One sultry evening early in July a young man emerged from the small furnished room he occupied in a large five-storied house in Sennoy Lane, and turned slowly, with an air of indecision, towards the Kalininsky Bridge. (*Crime and Punishment.* The author, by inserting "air of indecision," into a statement about a young man walking into the street, has raised the story question of what it is that he is indecisive about. It turns out, of course, that what he is indecisive about is committing murder.)

• News item from the Westover (Me.) weekly *Enterprise,* August 19, 1966:

> RAIN OF STONES REPORTED . . . It was reliably reported by several persons that a rain of stones fell from a clear blue sky on Carlin Street in the town of Chamberlain on August 17th. The stones fell principally on the home of Mrs. Margaret White, damaging the roof extensively and ruining two gutters and a downspout valued at approximately $25. . . . (*Carrie.* This opening raises all kinds of questions about this mysterious happening: What caused it? Why did the stones rain principally on this house? etc.)

• Scarlett O'Hara was not beautiful, but men seldom realized it when caught by her charm as the Tarleton twins were. (From *Gone with the Wind,* of course. The opening line obviously raises the story question of what are the consequences of the twins' having been charmed? Will they fight over her? And so on.)

Therefore, in the beginning of your damn good novel, right from the start, do as the masters do and open with a powerful story question and hook readers so strongly they cannot stop reading.

Webster's lists a second definition for suspense:

Suspense: n, 2. The state of being uncertain, as in awaiting a decision, usually characterized by some anxiety or apprehension.

Suspense in the first sense is a form of curiosity. The writer raises story questions the reader is curious about. In the second sense, the writer arouses more than just curiosity by putting the reader in a state of anxiety or apprehension. Suspense that makes the reader anxious or apprehensive is certainly more compelling than mere curiosity.

Now then, how do writers go about creating such a state? Consider the following:

> Mary was an inquisitive little toddler of eighteen months. She had bright blond curls, big blue eyes, and dimpled cheeks. She was just learning to walk and her mother was proud that she could stand by herself. She'd stand by the table and reach up and pull napkins and silverware off. She was always trying to find out what was "up there" above her, just out of reach, as if she were trying to find out just how this mysterious world works. And then one day her mother left a pot of water boiling on the stove when she went out of the kitchen for just a minute to answer the phone. Mary looked up and saw the brown and copper handle of the pot sticking out and she began to wonder about it. She crawled over to the stove and stood up, stretching her hand high for the handle . . .

In this case the story questions are: (1) Will little Mary reach the handle, pulling the pot off the stove, and will the boiling water scald her? and (2) Will the mother return in time? But the author's intention here is to do more than just raise story questions. Most readers will become anxious reading this, hoping a tragedy will be averted. Anxiety is a stronger response in the reader than curiosity.

To create apprehension and anxiety in the reader, the writer must first create a sympathetic character. A sympathetic character is one most readers will want to see good things happen to.

The next step in producing anxiety in the reader is to plunge the sympathetic character into a situation of menace. The menace does not have to be physical, of course. Consider the following:

> Little Prudence and Freddy Todd, hiding behind the barn, had concluded a deal whereby he could look up her skirt for exactly thirty seconds in exchange for two weeks' allowance. Old Aunt Matilda happened by and was a shocked witness to the fulfillment of this diabolical contract.

In this case, the menace is not physical, but is menace nevertheless. Social disapproval is often a greater consequence than physical menace. Think of this second type of menace as the reader's reasonable expectation that bad things are going to happen to a sympathetic character.

This applies not only in the opening. Throughout the story, the reader should be worrying about bad things that might happen to sympathetic characters.

- In *The Red Badge of Courage,* the bad thing is Henry's loss of courage and possible death.

- In *Jaws,* the bad thing is the great white shark that is eating sympathetic characters, and ruining Brody's life.

- In *Carrie,* the bad thing is what the awful boys at school have in mind for Carrie, and the even worse bad things that will happen to every sympathetic character in the town if they get her mad.

- In *Pride and Prejudice,* the bad thing is Elizabeth and Darcy not falling in love and marrying. (Even though they don't seem to get along, the reader knows they're meant for each other.)

- In *Crime and Punishment,* the bad thing is not Raskolnikov's contemplation of murder, but rather the dire consequences of that act.

- In *The Trial,* the bad thing is K.'s arrest.

- In *Gone with the Wind,* the bad thing is the coming of the Yankees.

How hard is it for a writer to set things up so that the dynamics of suspense—sympathetic character facing menace—are working? Not hard at all.

Say you work in an office and notice that everyone there seems to get ground down by the daily routine, and that as the years go by they get duller and duller, becoming zombielike drudges. You think that would be a wonderful thing to write about. You start your story. Every character in the story is getting ground down by the system, but there seems to be something wrong. No suspense. The menace is not there—not enough to induce a state of apprehension and anxiety in a reader. Okay, you ask yourself, *who* might be menaced? Certainly not one of the zombies. No, it would have to be a new employee. Someone who refuses to be ground down. Someone who will fight back.

You would also try to come up with what the menace might be. A boss in the office can't menace anyone easily, so you're stuck. You think, what if I changed the situation? What if it wasn't an office but a mental hospital, and the head nurse was determined to grind down a patient? You'd have a very suspenseful situation. In fact, it worked out quite well for Ken Kesey in *One Flew Over the Cuckoo's Nest.* It works because Big Nurse has the power to menace.

Say you have another idea for a story. There's a rich lady and her servant. She treats him like dirt. He takes her guff because he needs the job. You want to make some kind of statement about rich people's mistreatment of the poor, but where's the suspense? The menace? How about you put these characters on her yacht in the middle of the Mediterranean and it sinks. The rich lady and her servant make it to a deserted desert island. Now you've got a situation of menace; they must survive. No good? You didn't want to write a survival story?

How about the servant gets so fed up he decides to put on a disguise and meet the woman as an equal, and they fall in love? The menace? He might be found out and their love destroyed. Don't like that one either?

How about the servant finds out someone is trying to kill the rich lady and he does nothing but skulk around and get pictures of the conspirators? He may be menaced by the police—too late, he discovers they are planning to pin the crime on him.

Okay, you don't like crime stories. Fine. You want to tell quiet stories of "real people." You can still find menace. Jim Bob wants to marry Billy Jo. He proposes, she accepts. Your idea here is you want to show how people often get married because it's the thing to do, even when their partner isn't quite right for them. You create this small town in the Ozarks where girls get married at sixteen. You might have a great point to make, and there might be dire consequences down the road for Billy Jo, but they are too far off, too remote in time to create much suspense. The menace here is not immediate. To make it immediate, all you have to do is show that the marriage means Billy Jo will come to harm *now*. The harm does not have to be physical; it might simply mean her future is more uncertain. Say Billy Jo has a chance to study opera in Chicago. The marriage means she loses that opportunity. Now the prospect of the marriage has menace in it (loss of opportunity); consequently, the situation is more suspenseful.

Dean Koontz in *How to Write Best-Selling Fiction* (1981) said that "ninety-nine out of one hundred new writers make the same mistake in the opening pages of their books and it is one of the *worst* errors they could possibly commit: They do not begin their novels by plunging their hero or heroine into terrible trouble."

Menacing your character puts him or her in terrible trouble. If your character is sympathetic and menaced, you have created a state of anxiety and apprehension in the reader. Then the thing to do is light the fuse.

LIGHTING THE FUSE

This is one of the most potent techniques in creating suspense. What it means is this: Something terrible is going to happen, usually at an appointed time, and the characters must stop it from happening and that ain't easy.

In one of the "Perils of Pauline" movies, the hapless Pauline was tied down to the tracks by Snidely Whiplash and the 12:10 was never late. And Dudley Doright was meeting all kinds of obstacles to getting there on time.

In the Tarzan movies Jane was always clinging to a log or a capsized canoe and heading for the rapids. The Indiana Jones films have many similar situations.

The old TV show "Batman" made a parody of the lit fuse. Every week the dynamic duo were faced with a terrible end: being baked in a cake mix or sliced up under the blades of a huge pendulum or dangled over a vat of boiling acid while the rope unraveled.

Making up situations with a lit fuse is not difficult. Here are some examples:

• Lisa, who's been grounded by her parents, has snuck out to see a movie with her boyfriend and must be back at midnight when her parents get home. Trouble is, on the way home from the movies her boyfriend's car blows a head gasket...

• The sheriff has told Black Bart to get out of town by sundown, but Bart's not leaving, he says, and will kill anybody who tries to make him...

• A forest fire is heading toward the Brumble family, who are camping. Their car won't start. They've got to get out before the fire reaches them—and the wind is up...

• Doris Felcher has twenty-four hours to get an ounce of honey from the dreaded Albanian albino blood-sucking bee, or space aliens from Zork will destroy Earth...

• Little Mary has a high fever, and if ole Doc Adams doesn't make it through the blizzard in time...

Thriller writers know well the value of a lit fuse. In Frederick Forsyth's *The Day of the Jackal*, the Jackal is hired to kill Charles de Gaulle, the president of France, early in the story. The fuse is well lit; the hero must stop him in time.

In Ken Follett's *The Eye of the Needle*, the Nazi villain is trying to get to a radio to contact Berlin with critical information about the impending Normandy invasion. He must be stopped in time.

In the climactic sequence of *The Spy Who Came in from the Cold*, Leamas must get over the wall before the deadline or he'll be trapped behind the iron curtain.

It isn't only political thriller writers who use this technique.

- In *Jaws*, the shark must be killed before the closed beaches ruin the town's tourist industry and wreak untold hardships on the townspeople.

- In *The Red Badge of Courage*, after Henry runs, he discovers that because his unit was routed no one will know of his cowardice as long as he can get back in time.

- In *Gone with the Wind*, the Confederate Army is leaving Atlanta, the dreaded Yankees are coming to burn the city, and Scarlett must get out—but first she has to deliver Melanie's baby because the doctor has already fled.

- In *Carrie*, the fuse is lit as the pranksters are getting set to douse poor Carrie with pig's blood at the moment of her coronation as prom queen.

- In *Pride and Prejudice*, Lydia runs off to Gretna Green with Wickham and everyone's in a panic to catch up with them before she is completely ruined by the scoundrel.

Suspense, then, is a matter of creating story questions, putting the sympathetic characters in a situation of menace, and lighting the fuse. It is making the reader worry and wonder. *Who* the reader is worrying about, is, of course, the characters. If you're going to write a damn good novel, you're going to have to have damn good characters, which is the subject of our next discussion, in Chapter Three.

THREE

OF WIMPS AND WACKOS: CREATING TRULY MEMORABLE CHARACTERS

WIMPS

Most literary agents will tell you there is one type of story they don't ever want to see—even if it's beautifully written and set in an exotic Shangri-la. Crusty old editors recoil at the sight of them. Creative writing teachers often break out in hives when one of their students writes one. What is this dreaded monstrosity?

It's the *wimpy housewife* story.

Here is the usual scenario: A wimpy housewife who is a total klutz at everything—naive, ignorant, and yes, well, maybe even a little dumb—is stepped on by, that's right, her callous, nasty, and philandering husband.

The wimpy housewife does little about her problem except suffer for, oh, forty or fifty thousand words, until one day she's sparked into action, usually because a neighbor, friend, or therapist tells her she ought to, damn it, *do something*. Armed with this advice, the wimpy housewife, rather than confronting her problems, runs away to "find herself." She usually ends up having an affair with a married man, getting a job in a semiglamorous occupation such as advertising, journalism, top-of-the-market real estate, the arts. The wimpy housewife eventually learns to be self-sufficient, realizes that, yes, she too is a human being worthy of dignity, and finally makes it to the Top and marries Mr. Just Fine.

There's another version of this story, the *wimpy accountant*. The wimpy accountant is the male version of the wimpy housewife. He's a total klutz at everything—naive, ignorant, and yes, well, maybe even a little dumb—who is stepped on by, that's right, his callous, nasty, skirt-chasing boss. The wimpy accountant does little about his problem except suffer for, oh, forty or fifty thousand words . . .

You get the idea.

The problem with the wimpy housewife/accountant story is that even the potential market for the stories—wimpy housewives and wimpy accountants yearning to be free—will reject the story. Why? Because it's not possible to sympathize with a character who in the beginning is so wimpy that all he or she can do is suffer and wallow in self-pity. Such characters are what Edwin A. Peeples in *A Professional Storywriter's Handbook* (1960) calls "pathetic." He says we're contemptuous of pathetic characters "who do nothing but suffer, even if they do it stoically."

The wimpy housewife/accountant story fails because the wimpy protagonist is not worth reading about until the character has "found her/himself," and by then it's too late for the weary reader.

There is nothing wrong with starting out with a character who is a wimp. Nor is there anything wrong with having a character who is a housewife or an accountant. *Shirley Valentine* was an extremely successful novel, play, and film about a wimpy housewife. What made her interesting was that she was full of humorous and profound insights into her condition, and she did something about her plight—she fled to a Greek island and had a love affair.

The problem then, is not that a character is a wimp, but rather that he or she is, well, *constipated*. They cannot move. It is the constipated character that must be avoided. Create all the wimps you want, they can develop into giant killers and dragon slayers, but such characters won't grow unless they take actions and engage in conflicts. If they remain wimpy and constipated, you'll never be able to use them in your damn good novel.

To write a damn good novel, the main characters, wimps included, must become dynamic.

A dynamic character is driven. That is, the character, such as Shirley Valentine, wants something *desperately*. This desperation is the dynamo inside that fires up characters and pushes them into action.

Constipated wimps have only one dimension: They are long suffering. Dynamic characters have conflicting emotions and desires and are torn apart by strong emotions, such as ambition and love, or fear and patriotism, or faith and lust, or whatever. Inner emotional fires are raging; forces are pulling dynamic characters in more than one direction. Dynamic characters resolve these inner conflicts by taking actions that will lead to more story conflict and more inner conflict.

CHARACTERS WORTH KNOWING

Lajos Egri in *The Art of Creative Writing* (1965) asks rhetorically, "What should a writer strive for?" His answer: "Characterization. Living, vibrating human beings are still the secret and magic formula of great and enduring writing."

Vibrant, living, human beings are of course human beings that are worth knowing. Hamilton Clayton in *The Art of Fiction* (1939) says, "A novelist is, to speak figuratively, the social sponsor of his own fictitious characters; and he is guilty of a social indiscretion, as it were, if he asks his readers to meet fictitious people whom it is neither of value nor of interest to know."

What kind of characters are worth knowing intimately? Edwin A. Peeples says in *A Professional Storywriter's Handbook* that characters "must have the uniqueness of real people. They must have the contrasts of inconsistent behavior common to individuals . . . contrasts make character." It is through such contrasts that fully rounded, three-dimensional characters are brought to life. It is through contrast that good characters can become great characters who are truly worth knowing.

Great characters are so extraordinarily interesting that if you met them at a cocktail party you'd later want to tell others about them. A good dramatic character, then, is interesting in the normal sense of what makes people interesting.

Okay, so what is it that makes people interesting?

Some are interesting because they are well traveled. They've been to India, say, or Mozambique with the Peace Corps, or to the South Pole with *National Geographic*.

People are interesting who have thought deeply about life or who have strong, unusual opinions. Maybe they think they saw Elvis in a 7-Eleven. Maybe they voted for Prohibition, went ballooning in Algeria, or got arrested for throwing a snowball at a statue of Marx in East Germany in the bad old days. Interesting people have been places, they have done things, they have had rich and varied experiences. They have been on spiritual quests, they have been trying to unravel life's mysteries, they have, in other words, fully *lived.*

In *How to Write a Damn Good Novel* I advocated writing biographies for all the important characters, which is an extremely helpful practice. They help you make the characters real and multifaceted. But beyond that you should make the biographies interesting stories in themselves. Write biographies of characters who, if they were real people, might have real biographies written about them.

Okay, that's well and good, you say. But you've never been to India and sat at the foot of a transcendent guru, or played polo, or dined at the Château de Rothschild. So if you have not experienced it, how can you write about it?

Easy. The libraries are full of firsthand accounts of people who have done everything imaginable. When you create a boxer or a ballet dancer or a shark hunter, go to the library and poke around in a few biographies. You'll be amazed at what you find.

Say one of your characters is a whore. Any good library will have ten or fifteen life stories written by whores. The same goes for nuns, saints, jockeys, jocks, and submarine captains.

If you're writing about an actual accountant, the phone book is full of them. Call a couple and introduce yourself. Offer to buy them lunch and put them in your acknowledgments. Ask them what their on-the-job problems are, what joy they get out of work, how they got started in the business, what they want in the future. Have they caught any crooks, and what have they done about it? What do they think of the IRS?

Probe deeply; ask the tough questions. Just what does happen at an accountants' convention? How much dipping in the till never gets discovered? Can IRS auditors be bribed?

You get the idea. You want the nitty-gritty details of their lives.

You'll pick up attitudes and speech patterns that will make

your novel ring with the kind of authenticity, say, Joseph Wambaugh has in his. Even though Wambaugh was a cop for nearly twenty years, he still hangs out with cops, so he doesn't forget how they talk and act. Elmore Leonard says he does the same. Amy Tan knows intimately the Chinese immigrants to America whom she writes about with such insight. Joseph Wambaugh, Elmore Leonard, and Amy Tan are all writing damn good novels making use of their intimate knowledge.

Getting to know people like the ones you're writing about just might work for you, too.

CHARACTER AND COMPETENCE

Readers are intrigued by characters who are, as Aristotle says in the *Poetics*, "effective." In other words, they are good at what they do.

Detectives who are extraordinarily good at detecting are of far more interest than those who aren't (except when the detective's bungling is played for humor). Cowboy heroes are always good at drawing a gun, or twirling a lariat, or tracking, or some other skill. Homer knew this when he wrote the *Odyssey:* Ulysses was not only reckless and daring, but also a great sailor and a deadeye bowman. If you create competent characters, the reader will more easily identify with them.

• Brody in Peter Benchley's *Jaws* is extraordinarily good at being a sheriff. Hooper is an extraordinarily good marine biologist. Quint is an extraordinarily good shark hunter. The shark is extraordinarily good at attacking humans.

• Carrie's mother in Stephen King's *Carrie* is good at being a religious zealot. The pranksters who get Carrie elected prom queen are extraordinarily good at setting her up for the practical joke of the year. Carrie is extraordinarily good at being telekinetic.

• In Margaret Mitchell's *Gone with the Wind,* Scarlett is an extraordinarily good Southern belle—she knows how to flirt and flatter and get herself noticed, play one man off another—and Rhett Butler is an extraordinarily good gunrunner.

Great characters are often a little wacky. Some are even more than a little wacky, they're out there on the lunatic fringe.

Readers are charmed by wacky, *theatrical* characters. Wacky characters are often exaggerated, flamboyant, colorful, ditzy, dizzy, and contrary. When you think of the great characters of literature, who do you think of? Ahab in *Moby Dick* comes to mind. He's colorful, all right, and a little out there on the lunatic fringe. Zorba the Greek is one of the truly great wackos of all time. The modern novel was born, some scholars say, with the publication of *Don Quixote,* whose protagonist, jousting with windmills, was as wacky as they come. The English novel, some say, started with *Moll Flanders,* whose protagonist was a bit wacko, as well as a pickpocket and bigamist. Pierre Bezuhkov, one of the heroes of Tolstoy's *War and Peace,* is not, let us say, very tightly wrapped. He blunders onto a battlefield looking for philosophical truths.

In detective fiction, there's Hercule Poirot, who sleeps with a hair net and is exceedingly vain about his waxed mustache. Nero Wolfe raises orchids and never leaves his home. A little wacky, that, don't you think? How about Sherlock Holmes? He plays a violin all night and shoots up with morphine.

The creation of wacky characters is fun. One way is simply to take a trait and exaggerate it. A fanatical love of hamburgers, say. Or hatred of snakes, or bugs, or sharks. Or an obsessive love of Edsels, or electronic eavesdropping, or a compulsive need to examine tongues or put clothes on cats. Extremism in anything will serve.

Another way is to give the character a philosophy of life that is somewhat askew. Zorba the Greek believes in living life to the fullest, and damn the consequences. When asked where he worked last, he answers:

> In a mine I'm a good miner. I know a thing or two about metals. I know how to find the veins and open up galleries. I go down pits; I'm not afraid. I was working well. I was foreman, and had nothing to complain about. But then the devil took a hand in things. Last Saturday night, simply because I felt like it, I went off all of a

sudden, got hold of the boss, who had come that day to inspect the place, and just beat him up . . .

When asked what the boss had done to him, he answers:

> To me? Nothing at all, I tell you! It was the first time I saw him. The poor devil had even handed out cigarettes.

Now that is a deliciously wacky character.

Don't be afraid of wacky characters, no matter what kind of novel you're writing—even the most serious. Shakespeare made Falstaff a wonderful, wacky character in his serious history plays, *Henry IV Part One* and *Henry IV Part Two*. He's a coward and a drunk who belches skewed philosophy all over the stage. Vardaman Bundren in Faulkner's *As I Lay Dying* is a wacko: He's constantly repeating to himself "My mother is a fish," because, like his fish, she has just died. How about Joseph, the crusty old servant in Emily Brontë's masterpiece, *Wuthering Heights,* who's always cursing everyone and prophesying doom? Now there's wacky.

Wacky characters not only add spice to your story, they make a good contrast to your serious characters. In other words, they act as a foil. The use of foils is a literary device for enhancing the traits of one character by contrasting them with the totally opposite traits of another. In *Pride and Prejudice,* as an example, Darcy, Elizabeth's suitor, is a serious character who is contrasted with Elizabeth's sister Lydia's suitor, Wickham, a wacky con man. Hooper, the serious, scientific biologist in *Jaws,* is in sharp contrast to the wacky shark hunter, Quint. In *Carrie,* Carrie's mother is about as wacky a character as you'll find. She contrasts perfectly with the earnest, sincere, vulnerable Carrie.

Edwin A. Peeples in *A Professional Storywriter's Handbook* notes that Charlie Chaplin's use of contrasting the comic with the tragic "reaches an exquisite ultimate because [Chaplin's portrait of the little tramp] appears amid sadness, a sadness made almost unendurable because it is a background for outrageous humor. . . . He gives us short, violent contrast. It is this contrast that makes us remember."

You're taking risks, of course, when you create wacky characters, because they can go sour on you. They can come off as unbelievable, unsympathetic or, worse, silly. It's difficult to know whether you've put in enough spice, or too much. It's always a risky business.

But novelists, like race-car drivers, are in the risk-taking business.

CHARACTER CONTRAST AND SETTING

Characters should be contrasted not only with each other, but also with their setting. The rube coming to the city, for example. A socialite going to prison. Think of Mark Twain's *A Connecticut Yankee in King Arthur's Court*. The spoiled rich kid on a fishing boat in Rudyard Kipling's *Captains Courageous*. The hip street punk McMurphy in an insane asylum in Ken Kesey's *One Flew Over the Cuckoo's Nest*. The Kansas farm girl caught in a magical land in Frank L. Baum's *The Wizard of Oz*.

- In *Jaws,* Brody, the sheriff, hates the water; he can't even swim. Imagine putting such a character on a boat during a hunt for a man-eating great white shark about the size of a mobile home.

- In *The Red Badge of Courage,* the hero, Henry, is a terrified civilian-turned-army private who finds himself smack in the middle of the American Civil War.

- Scarlett in *Gone with the Wind* is a Southern belle, born and bred to be pampered. Imagine putting such a character in a war-ravaged country where she has to grub for roots to survive.

- In *The Trial,* K., the hero, is a rational man. Imagine how hard it is for him in the strange world of "The Law" where people are prosecuted for no reason at all.

- In *Crime and Punishment,* Raskolnikov, the intellectual, is thrown into the Russian prison system with professional killers and thieves.

- In *Carrie,* the innocent Carrie is asked to the prom by a boy in the elite clique. A strange world for her indeed.

To set your characters off and plunge them into immediate difficulties, put them someplace where they don't belong, where they're forced to deal with new and possibly frightening circumstances.

THE RULING PASSIONS

A ruling passion was defined in *How to Write a Damn Good Novel* as *a character's central motivating force . . . the sum total of all the forces and drives within him.*

The ruling passion defines the character for the writer; it enables the writer to bring the character to life with a phrase. The ruling passion might be to commit the perfect crime, or become a great preacher, or pickpocket, or art forger. It might be something less specific, like to be a good husband, or the ultimate couch potato, or simply to be left alone. Whatever it is, the ruling passion determines what the character will do when faced with the dilemmas he or she must overcome in the course of the story.

Take a character like, say, Spit Spalinski. His ruling passion: to be a great baseball relief pitcher, the next Goose Gossage. At the beginning of our story, Spit is trying out for teams, spending hours practicing his fork ball, and so on.

Suppose in Chapter Two Spit's brother, visiting from Milwaukee, is shot dead in Spit's hotel room, but before he dies he writes, *Why, Spit?* on the wall, so the cops think Spit did it.

Spit's ruling passion, to be the next Goose Gossage, will not be the prime motivating factor in this story. From the murder of his brother onward, Spit will devote every waking moment to proving his innocence and finding the real killer. The character's dramatic decision to change his passion ups the stakes and enhances his growth.

In Spit's case, then, he has one passion that rules his life, and another that rules the situation of the story. He has, in effect, a dormant and an active ruling passion. The dormant one still defines his character for the writer, but is not what motivates him once he is accused of murder. At all times characters must be driven by at least one ruling passion. At no time should they drift like cars without engines.

Okay, back to our story. In Chapter Five, say, Spit goes to California, driven by his new ruling passion to prove his innocence. He's in a creaky old apartment building when a tremblor hits. Spit's ruling passion to prove his innocence is forgotten. The one thing on his mind now: to save himself from falling masonry.

In other words, what motivates him in a particular scene may or may not be his original ruling passion, but he may return to it once the crisis is past. A character's ruling passion, then, is not necessarily constant; it may change in the course of a story and change back again. In many great stories, it is the switch from one ruling passion to another that forces dramatic decisions on the character and makes the reader root all the more for the character.

• Raskolnikov's ruling passion in *Crime and Punishment* is to escape from poverty, but after he commits murder, his ruling passion is to be spiritually redeemed.

• Henry's ruling passion in *The Red Badge of Courage* is to do his duty as a soldier, but as soon as the shooting starts, his passion is driving him to get the hell out of there. Later, his passion changes and he wants only to redeem himself.

• Carrie's ruling passion is to be like the other girls, symbolized by going to the prom. Once the mean boys and girls dump pig's blood on her as a prank at the moment she's crowned prom queen, her ruling passion is to use her psychokinetic powers to wreak vengeance.

• Scarlett O'Hara's ruling passion is to marry Ashley. When her plantation, Tara, is destroyed, her passion turns to rebuilding it.

• Elizabeth Bennet's ruling passion is her loyalty to her family, even to the point of turning down a marriage proposal from the highly eligible Mr. Darcy, who has a condescending attitude toward her family. But after she learns Darcy has saved her sister from ruin, she has a total change of heart, and her ruling passion then is marry him.

You will want to avoid changing the ruling passion too often, however. If you do, instead of having a damn good novel that is consistently well motivated and building dramatically toward a climax, you will have an antic novel that is just one damn thing after another.

When the core conflicts are resolved at the end of the story, the character may return to his or her original ruling passion, but often does not because of the changes, the dramatic growth, he or she has undergone. Spit, say, might realize at the end of the story that what he really loves is being a detective, and now that he's played a "real" game in the grown-up world, he's no longer interested in a kid's game like baseball. Besides, he has come to realize he never could have thrown a ball as hard as the Goose anyway.

If the character does return to his or her original ruling passion, it is often with a different outlook or understanding, which gives more meaning to the dramatic events of the story.

DUAL CHARACTERS

Some of the most memorable characters in literature have a dual nature. They are, in effect, two different and distinct characters living within one body.

Perhaps the most famous is Jekyll and Hyde.

Dual characters are conceived as such by the author right from the get-go.

Mary Wollstonecraft Shelley's Frankenstein monster was such a character: both a ferocious killer and a philosophy-loving gentle giant. Long John Silver was a cold-blooded pirate on the one hand, and a warm and loving father figure on the other. Darcy's aunt, Lady Catherine, was outwardly a stiff-necked society matron but, inside, a hopeless romantic. Carrie, of course, is a dual character: one side, a gawky teenager yearning for acceptance; the other, a young woman with terrible, godlike, psychokinetic power.

How do you create such characters? Think of them as being ego states. According to the psychological theory of transactional analysis popularized by Eric Berne in *Games People Play*, the ego exists in three distinct ego states, the *parent,* the *adult,* and the *child.*

When in the parent ego state, we say things like: "Wear your seat belt." In the adult ego state, we're rational beings—reflective and wise—and we say such things as: "I've made a list of all the reasons to build the new deck and feel we should, as it would add $15,000 in value to the house for a $12,800 investment." In the child ego state, we might try to get ahead of someone in traffic who tried to cut us off. "I'll teach him to cut me off!"

In creating a dual character, think of the ego states as going further than simply reflecting an attitude. Think of the ego states as being separate characters altogether, when in one ego state the character would say and do things he or she would never do in the other ego state.

Here's an example:

Suppose you have a character who's a major in the army in World War II. He's a brilliant tank commander, battle-hardened, tough, an astute tactician, fearless, gutsy, determined, ruthless, hard on his men; a by-the-book disciplinarian who will tolerate no disobedience to an order whatever.

Let's call him Major Broderick Rawlston. He's a pug-faced guy, chomping on a cigar, short, but broad-shouldered and immensely strong from lifting weights. A bulldog in soiled fatigues, two Colt .45 automatics swinging from his belt, he often carries a silver-tipped riding crop.

He was brought up in an army family: His father was in General Pershing's army in the First World War. He was taught from the time he could crawl that the highest duty on earth was to defend one's country. His ruling passion is to be the best damn tank commander in the whole damn army, bar none. If he has a flaw, it's that he drives his men, his tanks, and himself too hard. In his wake, he leaves a lot of dead Germans and a lot of spent shells . . . and a record number of cases of combat fatigue in his own ranks.

His men call him "Raging Rawlston." He's dramatic in every way. We could make a pretty interesting character out of him and his story would be well worth telling. But we could make an unforgettable character out of him if he had a dual nature.

Say Raging Rawlston as a child liked to draw pictures, which his military-minded parents thought was pretty silly stuff and did everything from bribery to ridicule to discourage. He didn't stop, though: He became a closet artist, painting in secret during stolen hours. In college, he frequented the local artists' colony and hung out with artists, never telling his military friends or his family. While hanging out with the artists, he was in his artist ego state: his usual pug face softened, the hard cast in his eyes disappeared, and he looked contemplative, serene.

By the time he's a forty-year-old major fighting Nazis he is long practiced in keeping his two natures separate. One of his dual personalities wants to be the greatest general; the other wants to create a masterpiece with oils on canvas. One side of him is iron hard, the other is pillow soft, yet both exist in the same man. When in his military ego state, he sees what his parents did for him as a good thing; in his artist ego state, he deeply resents it.

Raging Rawlston has a great potential as a character when we put him to a test to expose who he really is. Say he drives his tank through the wall of a church. To press the attack, he must drive his tank through another wall, on which he knows that a valuable Renaissance fresco is painted. His two selves would be at war with each other. Such a character could be well worth knowing.

Women characters may make good dual characters as well. Take Hilda O'Farrell. Let's say she's a society matron living on Nob Hill in San Francisco. She has a Pekingese with a rhinestone collar that sits on her lap all day. Born fabulously wealthy, Hilda was raised with the notion that she should shrewdly manipulate her holdings to increase them, which she does through her business manager.

Through and through a snob, she has her nose stuck pretty much in the stratosphere. She enjoys theater, ballet, and reading *Architectural Digest.* An avid bridge player, she's twice been on championship teams and finished second and third in the world invitationals. She detests disorder and has a fetish for cleanliness. If you wish to make the claim that you are somebody in San Francisco, you must be invited to Hilda's Sunday soirées. She's thirty-seven and has been through four husbands, all much older than she: All left her even more wealthy.

Now then, on to her dual nature.

Hilda is a practical joker. She can't help herself. Though she's a snobby socialite, she enjoys nothing more than seeing another snobby socialite made the butt of a practical joke. She realizes that her dual nature is incongruous, but that's the way it is; she just gets giddy sometimes and can't control herself.

Most of the time she's the snob, but sometimes a twinkle appears in her eyes and her other self takes over.

Hilda could be a very interesting character indeed. What if she married a presidential candidate? The king of England? The possibilities are awesome.

How about a more serious character? Let's call her Ivy Danforth, who in her younger days was the motherly sort. A gentle soul, a homemaker who loved children, a devoted wife to her husband, Dillon, a businessman—the wholesale plumbing-supply king. Ivy knew she was old-fashioned, but she was brought up to think of a woman's place as in the home, blah, blah.

Then Dillon keeled over from a heart attack and Ivy was thrust into the plumbing-supply business, which teetered on the brink of disaster. She took charge and saved the business, but in the process she had to become a hardheaded businesswoman, and did.

As our novel opens, at work she hires and fires and wheels and deals and has built the business into the largest plumbing-supply house on the planet, but at home she's still a mom who likes to bake fresh bread and knit sweaters. A woman with a dual nature.

The trouble comes at age forty-seven when, at the hospital to visit her daughter and new granddaughter, she meets Dr. Wayne Marlow, who is quickly enamored of her gentle ways, and love quickly blossoms. But will he be able to deal with her dual nature, of which he is not aware?

The possible complications are intriguing.

Here's another example:

Let's say there's a mild-mannered reporter for a great metropolitan newspaper. He's shy, timid, seemingly cowardly. Wears glasses. But he has a second nature: He's the man of steel, who wears his underpants on the outside, is faster than a speeding bullet, able to leap tall buildings with a single bound . . .

Remember "Kung Fu" on TV? Remember Caine? The hero was a dual character, a mild-mannered fellow, bowing and scraping and playing his flute, until provoked and then he became a tiger. How about *The Three Faces of Eve*, where three personalities inhabit one body. And the Godfather, Vito Corleone, who was a kind, loving father and a ruthless brutal gangster.

You get the idea.

To make your characters worth knowing, give them intriguing backgrounds, make them have unusual ideas and insights, let some of them be wacky, contrast them well with each other and their setting, maybe give them a dual nature. And take some risks with them, make them fresh.

And since your characters are going to change in the course of your damn good novel, you'll need to apply some advanced techniques of premise, which, as you might have guessed, is the subject of Chapter Four.

FOUR

THE "P" WORD (PREMISE) REVISITED

....

PART ONE: THE CONCEPT IS
EXPLAINED AND SIMPLIFIED

A ROSE BY ANY OTHER NAME
IS NOT A BANANA

The great pyramids in Egypt could not have been built without the invention of the chisel.

A chisel is a simple thing, nothing more than a piece of copper or bronze rod flattened at one end and sharpened. Yet the invention of this humble tool is what led to the building of those colossal monuments. Without the chisel those huge edifices would be just piles of rocks.

Premise is the fiction writer's chisel. It's the simple tool that helps shape your fictional material and create a colossal monument—a damn good novel.

There is no more powerful concept in fiction writing than that of premise. If you structure your stories with a strong premise in mind, your novel will be well focused and dramatically powerful, and it will hold your readers from beginning to end.

As I explained in *How to Write a Damn Good Novel*, premise is a *statement of what happens to the characters as a result of the core conflict of the story*. The "core conflict" is simply another way of saying the *actions* of the story. That's what a premise is. It's a *statement of what happens to the characters as a result of the actions*

49

of the story. That's it. What could be simpler? Yet once you have articulated your premise, you will be able, as if by magic, to shape your fictional material the way a stonemason shapes a stone with a chisel.

Many beginning writers have a great deal of difficulty grasping this concept. Perhaps the word itself, *premise,* sounds like a word that would be used by mathematicians and symbolic logicians, geniuses who write brain-numbing symbols in long chains on blackboards. Perhaps it would be better if, instead of *"premise,"* a more user-friendly term were used, like *story statement,* or *story summary.* Or *writer's banana,* something like that. Unfortunately, that would only make things more confusing; there's already a blizzard of terms being used and no more are needed.

When I was learning the craft, my mentor, Lester Gorn, would ask me what my premise was for every story I wrote, and for years I'd fumble and mumble and say something like "You shouldn't lie," or "Living leads to dying," or "Never trust a stranger." He'd get red in the face and tell me I wasn't in control of my work and then he'd tell me what my premise was, but even when I knew it I couldn't use it because I didn't know how.

In the classes I teach, as soon as I mention the word *premise* I can see many of my students' eyes glaze over. After all, they're creative people: Why should they have to have some controlling principle in their stories? Isn't it more fun just to let the characters write the story?

It may be more fun, but it's the road to disaster. As novelists, we create fiction out of what DeVoto in *The World of Fiction* calls "a stream of revery" and the "novelist's gift for fantasy" and the "ability to organize his fantasies in coherent sequences." Organizing the fantasy into a coherent sequence is what you do when you form a premise and set out to prove it.

Sure, it's great to go with the flow of the fantasies and the reverie, but that's exactly where the problem lies. If you don't know your premise, your characters *will* write the story, but what story will they write? You might get lucky—it might turn out to be a good one. But I've noticed with my students, and they are a very talented lot indeed, that the chances of coming up with a damn good story by letting the characters do what they will is about one in a hundred. Without a premise, the writer has no blueprint. Without a premise, it is as if you're starting out on a trip to Kansas from

New York, blindfolded. Without a premise, you're simply imitating life, with all its boring byways and blind alleys.

A premise is *a brief statement of what happens to the characters as a result of the actions of the story.* Embodied in the statement is, as Lajos Egri says in *The Art of Dramatic Writing,* "character, conflict and conclusion."

Once a fiction writer is able to articulate the premise, he or she can use it as a test for each complication, asking, Is this really necessary to proving the premise? When the story is finished, the writer can then ask, Is the premise proved by the actions of the story?

Gerald Brace, in *The Stuff of Fiction* (1969), points out that "in the ideal dramatic fiction everything is relevant, everything counts, everything leads on to what is to come . . . and at the inevitable climax, all is resolved and settled for good or ill."

Nothing will help you get closer to this ideal than knowing your premise.

FINDING A PREMISE FOR A PARTICULAR STORY

Bernard DeVoto in *The World of Fiction* says that the best teacher of creative writing he has ever known, Miss Edith Mirrielees, always began a discussion of a student's story by asking, "What is this story *about?*"

This is the most important question fiction writers can ask themselves about their stories. It is the first step toward finding the premise.

Once you know what the story is about, you will be able to say, "Here is my truth: Human nature is such that, given a particular set of characters tested by a particular set of conflicts, the course of events will change human beings in this particular way."

Your premise is an abbreviation of what your story says. It is your truth, your vision; it is what you're communicating about human nature and the human condition.

As a creative writing teacher, I see new writers come into my classes with fictional material they feel very strongly about, but they just can't shape it into a story. The reason is, they don't know what their story is *about*.

When I was starting out, I took the advice often given to beginners—write what you know about! What I knew about was being an automobile claims adjuster, so I started hammering out a biographical literary novel called *The Cockroach*.

The hero (me) was working in a job he hated, surrounded by people who were hopelessly bogged down in the mundane details of life. He longed for release through artistic expression. He got involved with union organizing, consulted spiritualists, went to a marriage counselor. The guy was a mess. He kept making the same mistakes, went here, went there, got drunk, wrecked his car, got fired, got a new job, had an affair—in short, he was bobbing around like a cork adrift in a typhoon.

My mentor kept asking me what this novel was about. What was the premise? And I kept staring at him blankly, mumbling that it was about being a claims adjuster.

My story should have been about *some* aspect of human life, not *all* aspects. *All* aspects of human life is too broad a subject. In fiction, we put one or two aspects of life under our microscope, subject them to an experimental treatment called conflict, and then document what happens. A good dramatic story is a laboratory of human nature. It says something about some aspect of human life that the author believes deeply. If you're going to write a damn good novel, you have to believe deeply that what you are saying about human nature, human values, human existence is true, given the particular circumstances of the story.

You may not be as fortunate as I have been; you may not find a great mentor as I did. You will then have to do for yourself what my mentor did for me. Every time you sit down to write, ask yourself what the story is about.

Okay, say it's a story of love. The only kind of love worth writing about is some kind of powerful love, whether it's filial, brotherly, romantic, lustful, obsessive, whatever. The answer to the question of what the story is about will give you the first part of your premise. What happens to the character, as a result, will give you the rest of it. In a story of obsessive love, say, the love becomes overbearing to the protagonist's lover and the protagonist loses her in the end and kills himself. *Obsessive love leads to suicide* is the premise of the story.

Once you have the premise, you know everything. You know, as an example, that the conflict with the protagonist's grandmother has nothing to do with the obsessive love and doesn't contribute to the suicide. You know that the loneliness that leads to the obsessive love does belong in the story. You now know where you're going.

Don't like a suicide in the end? How about: Obsessive love leads to something else? Say, spiritual enlightenment or blissful happiness? Your premise is yours alone; it's your truth, your vision, it's the way things work out in the world you've created.

SORTING OUT THE BABBLE OF TERMS

There's a great deal of confusion among fiction writers as to how a premise differs from a *moral,* or a *theme.*

The easiest to understand is a moral. A moral is simply what a story teaches. Army training films about sexually transmitted diseases have a moral: *If you don't protect yourself, you might catch something horrible.* Bible stories often have morals: *Obey God's laws or suffer the consequences.* A fable has a moral: *Look before you leap,* or *Never trust a fox.* Fairy tales often teach that if you don't listen to your parents, you could get into bad trouble with bears or wolves or wicked witches.

Fiction writers are artists, not moralists. A damn good novel does not have a moral in the sense that an army training film, a Bible story, a fable, or a fairy tale does. If you wrote a story, however, where love fails to save an alcoholic, you could say the novel has a moral: *Never love a drunk.* And most detective novels probably have the moral *Crime doesn't pay.* But that doesn't mean that the author's purpose in writing a detective novel is to preach a sermon about the evils of the act of murder, nor that people read detective novels for moral edification.

In modern fiction, if a novel has a moral it's probably coincidental. As an example, a single-story novel might have as its premise *Alcoholism leads to spiritual growth,* and its moral might be *Drinking gets you closer to God,* which would certainly not be a moral in the traditional sense. Alcoholism is supposed to lead to degradation and death. In traditional stories religion or right moral action would lead to spiritual enlightenment, but in modern novels religion often leads to some sort of perdition, such as incest or madness. In other words, in the modern novel the moral is the opposite of what was traditionally thought of as a moral. Often, modern novels have an *immoral* moral, in the traditional way of seeing things, like *Don't tell the truth, it will wreck your marriage* or *Committing murder is a growth experience.* But we don't read to improve our morals much anymore.

Okay, so much for a moral, which has to do with teaching a moral lesson. Neither a theme nor a premise is intended to teach a moral lesson.

A lot of confusion has been created by the authors of how-to-write books about the definitions of theme and premise, so much so that they've become *weasel* words. They can mean one thing to you, another thing to me, and something else to a third party, and we'd all be right. If none of us is willing to accept a definition other than our own, we're stuck in the Tower of Babel and we'll never get down to writing a damn good novel.

For the purposes of this book, let's settle on a definition for each. It really doesn't matter if you call a premise a premise and a theme a theme, or you call a premise a banana and a theme a nork; it's the concepts that are important.

Dean Koontz defines theme in *How to Write Best-Selling Fiction* as "a statement or a series of related observations about one aspect or another of the human condition, interpreted from the unique viewpoint of the author." John Gardner says pretty much the same thing in *The Art of Fiction:* "by *theme* here we mean not 'message'—a word no good writer likes applied to his work, but to the general subject, as the theme of an evening of debates may be World-Wide Inflation."

Okay? A theme is a recurring fictional idea. A novel might explore the following ideas: the differences between, say, filial love and carnal love; what it means to have true courage; duty to an insane mother or a brother who is a criminal; how one stands up to impending death or a crippling disease. These recurring fictional ideas are themes.

For the purpose of our discussion, themes are defined as *recurring fictional ideas, aspects of human existence that are being tested or explored in the course of the novel.* A premise, which is *a statement of what happens to the characters as a result of the actions of a story,* is neither a moral or a theme.

Now that we have the terminology straight, we can get down to specifics.

PREMISES AT WORK

Let's take a look at some specific premises and how they work. We'll begin with a story we're all familiar with:

> A mama pig has three little pigs. One day the mama pig decides they're old enough to make it on their own, so she sends them into the world with a little money to build their own houses. To save money for things more frivolous than strong building materials, the first pig builds his house of straw and the second builds his of sticks. The third pig builds his house of bricks. When the bad wolf comes along, he quickly blows down the first two houses and devours their residents, but when he comes to the third, he can't. So the wolf tries climbing down the chimney, but the pig has a pot of boiling water waiting, traps the wolf, and has wolf stew for dinner.

What would the premise be? Simple: *Foolishness leads to death and wisdom leads to happiness.*

In other words, the *subject* of this story (what it is about) is foolishness and wisdom. This story is *not* about home construction. Home construction is the arena in which the real story is being told. The building of the houses, the actions of the story, make up the *text* of the story. Wisdom and foolishness is the *subtext* of the story, and it's the subtext that is the true subject of a story. The actions of the story (the text) prove the premise of the story (the subtext).

Instead of houses, the pigs could have built boats or airplanes or anything, and the subtext would have been the same. The actions prove that the first two pigs are foolish and the third pig is wise.

Having articulated the premise, the writer must ask whether there are any actions in the story that do not add to the proving of the premise. Are there any irrelevant actions in "The Three Little Pigs"? There don't seem to be.

Next, the writer should ask himself or herself whether the events of the story adequately prove the premise. The foolish pigs die and the wise pig gets to eat a fine boiled wolf dinner. Okay, the premise is proven.

Say there was an incident where the pigs go to the fair and meet some lady pigs, can't get a date, and go home and get drunk. Would that have anything to do with proving the premise? Nope. So out it would go.

What if there were a few actions showing the pig that built the straw house escaping and killing the wolf by shooting it with a .44 Magnum? Wouldn't have anything to do with wisdom and foolishness, would it? What if a scene or two showed the first pig losing his first house to a hurricane and building a second one out of mud? It would be redundant in proving of the premise; therefore, not needed.

Beginning fiction writers often feel that articulating a premise somehow puts a straitjacket on their creativity. Nothing could be further from the truth.

What happens if a writer does not know his or her premise? The story often disintegrates into a series of random events that has no development and the reader quickly loses interest.

When you begin a novel or start to watch a movie, there is a period when you don't quite know what the story is about. Say a novel goes like this: In the opening situation, Mary Beth is fighting with her mother over going to a school dance, and finally convinces her mother to let her go. At this point, what is the story about? Well, it could be a relationship story, but we can't really tell.

Okay, Mary Beth goes to the dance, and there she meets Fred, who she thinks is a nice boy, but he has an odd glint in his eyes and we think he may be dangerous. Ah, we think, this might be a story about a girl falling for a boy who's possibly dangerous. Maybe there's a murder about to happen.

She goes to a party after the dance with the boy, but he goes off with another girl and Mary Beth has to walk home alone. On the way, she meets a bag lady, who walks along with her . . .

The reader begins to feel lost in a maze, as if he or she is being told about an afternoon at the zoo by a four-year-old. Things happen, but we can't tell what the story is about and it is very frustrating. A story with a premise has a subject and a developing situation that leads to some sort of resolution.

One dead giveaway that a story is not about anything, that it doesn't have a subject and therefore is not developing, is to ask yourself whether the incidents of the story can be reordered without changing the story. If Mary Beth can meet the bag lady before the boy at the prom, chances are the story has poor development. In a story with a good development, the incidents cannot be moved around because the situation keeps changing and they would play differently if they were in any other place.

Knowing your premise is like having a cannon to stuff the gunpowder of your creativity into. Without a premise, no matter how much gunpowder you've got, you may have a lot of flash and smoke, but you won't blow down any walls.

A MIGHTY EXAMPLE

Let's take a look at another story we're all familiar with. Samson and Delilah. If you don't know the story, you can find it in the Book of Judges in the Bible.

The way it's told here is not exactly the way it's told in the Bible. This is more like the version told by Hollywood, in the 1951 epic starring Victor Mature and Hedy Lamarr. Let's call it the damn good version.

Samson and Delilah is the story of a man who is loved by God and given superhuman strength, becomes a hero in battle, is corrupted by carnal love, and loses his superhuman strength, whereupon he repents, his strength is restored, and he achieves a great victory over his enemies, dying in the process.

What would Samson's premise be? How about *Repentance leads to a glorious death?*

When you make a story statement such as *Repentance leads to a glorious death,* what you are really saying is: God's love leads to great strength, which leads to heroism in battle, which leads to haughtiness and arrogance, which lead to temptations of the flesh, which lead to betrayal, which leads to defeat and disgrace and blindness, which lead to repentance, which leads to a restoration of superpowers, which leads to a glorious death. The premise *Repentance leads to a glorious death* is just a shorthand way of stating it.

In other words, a premise says that *through a causal chain of events, one situation will lead to another and will eventually lead to a resolution.*

Here's how we'll prove the premise of our damn good version:

THE PROLOGUE: An angel visits Samson's mother, who's been barren, and tells her she will have a child—a Nazarite, a blessed child. (This shows that Samson is special, that he's loved by God.)

THE OPENING INCIDENT: Samson is a young man, on his way to town to court a woman. He meets a lion and tears it apart, "as a man tears a kid." (Shows how brave and strong he is.)

THE INCITING INCIDENT (the event that comes into everyday life that brings the change and starts the chain of events of the story): Samson is about to marry a Philistine woman. There's a little fracas at the wedding feast and the bride's father takes the bride back, so Samson sets fire to the Philistine's cornfields. (To show how the trouble starts.)

FIRST COMPLICATION: The Philistines—3,000 strong—come over to the Israelites' camp, seeking revenge on Samson. Samson, with the now famous jawbone of an ass, kills 1,000 of them. (To show how mighty Samson is, advancing the plot.)

SECOND COMPLICATION: The Philistine king is beside himself with anger. He orders an army of 10,000 raised to teach this punk a lesson. But Delilah, a gorgeous call girl, convinces the king he can save a lot of dough by sending her instead. (To show she's greedy.)

THIRD COMPLICATION: Delilah shows up and introduces herself to Samson. He falls for her wiles. (Showing how he starts to go bad.)

FOURTH COMPLICATION: Samson becomes a lush. (Shows how Delilah corrupts him.)

FIFTH COMPLICATION: Delilah has fallen for the poor slob, so she goes to the Philistine king and exacts his promise not to harm Samson if she's able to get his secret. (Nice dramatic growth on her part.)

SIXTH COMPLICATION: Delilah tries to wheedle the secret of Samson's great strength out of him. (His resistance shows he still has a shred of loyalty to his God.) But she finally manages to learn that it's his hair!

SEVENTH COMPLICATION: She cuts his hair; he loses his strength. (Shows his fall from grace.) The Philistines take him prisoner.

EIGHTH COMPLICATION: The Philistine king keeps his word and does not draw his blood, but puts a hot poker in his eyes and blinds him, then ties him to a grinding wheel.

NINTH COMPLICATION: Delilah, horrified, begs for forgiveness. Samson gives it, and begs forgiveness from God. Gradually his hair grows back. (Shows Samson's return to God.)

TENTH COMPLICATION: The Philistines, having a celebration, bring Samson to their temple to mock him. Delilah leads Samson to the building's main support pillars, which he pushes over, killing his enemies and gaining his glorious death. (The premise is proved: Repentance leads to a glorious death.)

We've shown how Samson came to be loved by God, how strong he was, how he got corrupted, how he lost his strength, how he repented, and how he achieved his glorious death.

You could also say this is the story of a man corrupted by lust who repents and achieves a glorious death, because it's a causal chain of events. Or you could say that the premise is *Being chosen to be a hero by God leads to a glorious death,* and you'd be just as correct. Either way, the meaning is the same; the same chain of events occurs to prove the premise because the premise is a *shorthand* way of stating what the chain of events is that leads the characters through conflict to the conclusion.

TYPES OF PREMISES

There are three types of premises: (1) chain reaction, (2) opposing forces, and (3) situational.

The *chain reaction* type of premise is the simplest to understand. Something happens to the character that sets off a series of events, leading to some kind of climax and resolution.

In this kind of story, something unexpected usually happens in the beginning. Say you have Joe Average on his way to work one day, hating his humdrum life, when he sees an armored truck career around the corner and a bag fall out the back door. Joe picks the bag up, takes it home, and finds that it contains $3 million. His wife pressures him to turn it in; he does, and becomes a celebrity. He goes on the "Tonight Show," where he talks about his great love of dogs (which he made up because he felt he had to say something) and is picked up as a spokesman for dog food, so he becomes even more of a celebrity and a champion of animal rights.

Joe begins to get a swelled head. His wife leaves him and sues for a ton of money in the divorce. He starts living high on the hog, gets taken to the cleaners by a succession of girlfriends, and starts drinking. While staggering home one night, he encounters a dog on the street and kicks it to make it get out of his way. His mistreatment of the dog is videotaped and put on all the news shows. He's ruined. In the end Joe gets his old job back, realizes fame was not for him, remarries his ex-wife, and is perfectly happy.

Premise: *Finding a bag of money leads to perfect happiness.* This premise is a shorthand way of saying: This is the story of a guy who finds a bag of money, goes on the "Tonight Show," becomes a spokesman for a dog food commercial, gets famous, turns into an arrogant jerk, loses his wife, is spotted kicking a dog and loses it all, and gets his wife and old job back and is perfectly happy. Stating the premise as *Finding a bag of money leads to perfect happiness* is a more concise and more eloquent way of saying the same thing.

The *opposing forces* type premise describes a story where two forces are pitted against each other and one wins. *Love defeats patriotism*, as an example, might be the premise of the story of a young man in the German army who falls in love with a Czech woman and turns on his country. Perhaps it is a tragic story where *Alcoholism defeats love* or where *Greed destroys idealism.*

You could express an opposing forces premise as an equation, x vs. y = z. *Love of country vs. love of God yields death,* as an example. Or it could be *Carnal love vs. duty to family yields suicide.* Or *Carnal love vs. greed yields ecstasy.*

How would you prove the premise *Alcoholism destroys love*?

You might start by showing that Joe loves Mary. He's so crazy about her he defies his family to marry her. He wins her from a rich guy, which proves she really loves him. Then Joe starts drinking, for fun. Driving drunk, he has an accident, and Mary is hurt. She forgives him. He tries to quit drinking. Mary starts seeing another man. Joe finds out. They fight. He swears off drink forever. They move to another city and put the past behind them. Joe's new job has a lot of pressure: He just has to have a drink to calm his nerves. Mary finds his hidden bottles. She returns to her lover and Joe is left with his bottle, heading for skid row.

Okay, so it's not a great story and there aren't a lot of surprises, but it clearly shows that *Alcoholism destroys love.*

A *situational* premise is where some situation is affecting all the characters. Joseph Wambaugh's novels are often about what being a cop does to human beings. Some, it ennobles; some, it destroys. Many war novels examine the effects of war on human beings. The same pattern fits prison novels, novels of poverty, novels of the religious life, and so on.

A situational premise can get away from an author easily, because it can get out of focus. Since each character has his or her own arc (that is, they will change in different ways as a result of being in the situation), it's useful to look at a situational novel as many stories, each with its own premise, that belong between the same cover because all the stories are affected by the same situation.

Let's say we're going to write a novel about the Civil War.

In our novel, Lieutenant Smith, an innocent, tender guy, is driven insane. His premise: *War drives a tender innocent insane.* Sergeant Brown, a hard man, becomes a brute. His premise: *War brutalizes.* Private Jones, a dreamer and poet, ends up bitter. His premise: *War embitters.* General Fitzgibbons, a bold tactician, is crushed and killed. His premise: *Foolhardiness leads to doom.* This is not to say that every character ends up badly. Corporal Natz, the medic, a morose loner, becomes a hero. His premise: *Heroism leads to self-satisfaction.*

We have defined moral, theme, and premise, and shown the three types of premises and how they work. In the next chapter, we'll take a look at how to use a premise like a magic wand to explore the implicit possibilities of your story.

FIVE

THE "P" WORD (PREMISE) REVISITED

....

PART TWO: THE NOVELIST'S
MAGIC WAND

PREMISE PRESTIDIGITATION

Let's examine a story and see how, if we change the premise, the story changes. A simple trick indeed. Here's our story:

> Joe, an idealistic young man, inherits his grandfath-
> er's farm, which he is determined to make totally organic.
> To his horror, he finds some of his neighbors reaping
> huge profits by making illegal pesticides. He pretends to
> be one of them and in the end brings them to justice.

The premise for this story: *Courageous idealism leads to victory over evildoers.*

So, this is a story *about* courageous idealism. What happens to the protagonist as a result of his courageous idealism? He is victorious. To write the story of Joe's courageous idealism leading to victory over evildoers you might construct a stepsheet that outlines the progression of events like this:

THE OPENING SITUATION: Joe is in some sort of conflict over his idealism—say he's reading his poetry on the street and the cops want him to move on; he sticks by his rights and gets arrested. (You're showing he's idealistic and is willing to stick to his ideals.)

THE INCITING INCIDENT: Returning home from paying his fine, he learns he owns the farm.

FIRST COMPLICATION: He takes over the farm, determined to make it organic. He sweats a lot, finds a lot of satisfaction. (You're showing his idealism at work on the farm and you've proven at least to some degree his commitment.)

SECOND COMPLICATION: He's shocked to discover his neighbors making and using illegal pesticides that poison the groundwater. (You're introducing the evildoers.)

THIRD COMPLICATION: Determined to put an end to their evil ways, he gets together with the local police to infiltrate the illegal pesticide underground. (You're putting his idealism to a stronger test.)

FOURTH COMPLICATION: Joe joins his neighbors in their nefarious activities, faces dangers, and finally gets the goods on the bad guys. (You're showing him being courageous.)

FIFTH COMPLICATION: The bad guys try to kill Joe; he's terrified, but sticks to his mission. (You're putting his idealism to the ultimate test, upping the stakes.)

THE CLIMAX: The bad guys are brought to justice.

THE RESOLUTION: Joe returns to his farm. The community is grateful and he feels fulfilled. (You're showing he triumphs.)

Having completed your plan for proving the premise, you need to ask yourself some hard questions:

- Is the premise proved? Answer: Yes. You've shown that idealism leads to triumph.

- Are there any superfluous complications? Answer: No.

- Are there ironies and surprises? Answer: Well, no, not really.

- Do the characters grow and develop? Answer: Gee, no, not very much.

- Is the story worth writing? Answer: Hell no!

If there are no ironies and surprises and the characters don't develop, it's obvious the story is not worth writing.

Okay then, using the same character in the same situation, how might the story statement be changed to make the story more ironic and dramatically powerful and give the character more development?

First, let's cut out the melodrama of the neighbors making illegal pesticides as part of an underground conspiracy that he infiltrates. Let's say Joe inherits the farm, but his scheme to make it organic doesn't work. Gradually, economic factors force him to first use legal pesticides, then illegal ones, then dangerously illegal ones. Okay, we get out our magic wand and try a new premise: *Economic necessity destroys idealism.* The sequences of events would go like this:

THE OPENING SITUATION: As before, Joe, a young poet, has a conflict over the reading of his poetry on the street. The police want him to move on; he sticks up for his rights and is arrested. (You've shown him to be idealistic.) Because he refuses to plead guilty and pay a five dollar fine (thus again proving his idealism, and impracticality as well), he is sentenced to a weekend in jail.

THE INCITING INCIDENT: Joe inherits his grandfather's farm.

FIRST COMPLICATION: He takes over the farm, determined to make it organic. Through sweat, he finds satisfaction in converting the farm from chemical farming to organic farming. Struggling to do it right, he overcomes many obstacles to getting his crops started. Neighbors jeer him. He has some initial success—the peach crop looks good—but he worries: There are so many things that could go wrong. (His commitment is proven.)

SECOND COMPLICATION: Nasty bugs attack his crop. He manages to turn them back partially using organic means. He saves half his crop of peaches and sells the rest of it for jelly. Rains ruin his watermelons. He's discouraged. (The forces of nature are allied against him.)

THIRD COMPLICATION: Payments on loans and taxes drain his resources. The banks refuse to extend credit to a dreamer such as Joe. They're sure he's going to fail. In desperation, he uses legal pesticide to save his strawberries. (You've shown Joe's idealism starting to crack.)

FOURTH COMPLICATION: Once having used a pesticide, he finds it easier to use it again. And when pesky crickets threaten and legal pesticides fail, Joe turns to illegal ones. This endangers the groundwater, but he feels forced to take the risk, letting the illegal pesticide maker convince him of the pesticide's safety. (The crack in his idealism grows larger.)

THE CLIMACTIC CONFRONTATION: The killer bees are coming. Nothing can stop them but a dangerous illegal pesticide. It means financial ruin if he doesn't use the pesticide, and ruin for the environment if he does. He uses the pesticide.

THE RESOLUTION: Joe saves his crop, but loses his soul and falls into despair.

Now, once again, we have to ask ourselves:

- Is the premise proved? Answer: Yes.

- Are there any superfluous complications? Answer: No.

- Are there ironies and surprises? Answer: Yes.

- Do the characters grow and develop? Answer: Yes.

- Is the story worth writing? Answer: Let's give it a qualified yes.

Okay, we've improved the story a great deal by using the magic wand of premise.

We could complicate this story even more by getting out our magic wand once more and creating a love interest. Perhaps it's for love that he caves in to using the illegal pesticides. Then the premise would be *Love destroys idealism*, far more fresh and interesting.

The fictional subjects of the story, then, would be love and idealism. Farming would still be the text. This same story can be told if the idealistic young man inherits a tuna boat and economic forces drive him to use illegal gill nets. Or if he inherits a grocery store and economic factors drive him to sell alcohol to teenagers. The text would change; the premise would not.

PREMISE-MAKING FOR FUN
AND PROFIT

One night you have a terrible nightmare. In the nightmare you've committed a heinous crime and the law is closing in on you. You awake in a sweat and decide, wow, that would make a damn good novel. The nightmare is your germinal idea. You plan to write a novel about a man who commits a murder and feels the law closing in on him.

This is not a premise. This is simply an *idea* for a story; so far we have no story at all.

Okay, the next day you sit down at your word processor and type "Notes" and then start throwing thoughts at your germinal idea. Who is you main character? Why does he commit the murder? And so on. What you want to write about is an average man who commits murder. He's not at all the murdering type—he does it for noble reasons, perhaps. He does it to protect his family, say.

That's good. But what is the noble reason?

You don't know. You brainstorm it, but can't come up with anything.

Then you read an article in the paper about a stalker, a man who supposedly loved woman and stalked her and when she shunned him, he killed her. The woman had gone to the police, but what could they do? They couldn't protect her twenty-four hours a day. She obtained a court order, but the stalker ignored it, and when she dragged him into court, he got a slap on the wrist.

That's good, you think. That would certainly motivate a murder. The average man's wife is being stalked and the courts and the police can't stop it, so the hero decides he has every moral right to kill the stalker.

You now have a beginning, but you still don't have a premise. Why? Because a premise includes an ending to the story. Knowing your premise means that you know what happens to the characters as a result of the actions of the story.

Okay, so the husband commits the murder and gets rid of the body, and the police start closing in on him. Now, what aspect of human existence are we going to focus on in this story? What is our story about? Here are some possibilities:

1. This could be a detective story, where the average man could be the killer and a cop, the hero.

2. It could be an American version of *Crime and Punishment,* where the focus would be on the killer's remorse: in other words, a story of repentance and spiritual transformation.

3. It could be a love story, where the killer is crazy about his wife and can't live with the idea that she might be harmed, but once he kills for her and she finds out, she's horrified to be around him. The story would end with irony: He loses the love he kills for.

4. It could even be a comic story of a man who is trying to kill a stalker and keeps missing.

5. Or it could be a story of betrayal, say, where the wife makes the husband think she is being stalked to get him to murder someone so he'll be sent to prison and she'll be rid of him.

So which one do you choose? These kinds of choices are mostly subjective. If you choose number one, the protagonist would be the detective and the story would have the usual detective story premise: *The determination and deductive skill of the detective hero bring justice.* The focus would be on the clever and resourceful way the killer would commit the crime and the even more clever and resourceful way the hero detective would go about solving the crime.

Number two, the American *Crime and Punishment* story, would have another focus altogether. You'd examine the life of a killer in terms of his guilts and repentance. It would be a psychological novel in which the detective would probably have an easier time bringing the murderer to justice, but the novel would not end there; it would continue, focusing on the transformation of the killer's life. The premise would be something like *The act of murdering leads to spiritual enlightenment.*

In number three, the story of the man who kills for love where the act of murder destroys the very thing he kills for, the premise would be: *Obsessive love leads to loss of love.*

Number four, the comic story, would probably have a comic ending. The premise? *Attempted murder leads to happiness,* perhaps.

The last story, number five, might end with the wife going off with her lover, but the lover, knowing what a betrayer she is, betrays her. The premise of this story might be *Betrayal of love leads to love betrayed.*

Any of these, depending on how it is handled, can be made into a damn good novel. The one I like best is number three: *Obsessive love leads to loss of love.* Why, I don't know. It's subjective: I just have the feeling deep in my gut that I could make a damn good novel out of it.

So how would such a premise be proved? Easy:

THE OPENING SITUATION: Jules (our hero) comes down to breakfast. His wife, Jo Ann, is at breakfast. She came home late the night before and he wonders where she was. She says she was working late (she's a real estate broker). He's so in love with her that she placates him easily. (This shows his excessive love.)

THE INCITING INCIDENT: A friend at work (in an insurance office) tells Jules he saw his wife going into a motel the night before. Jules sticks up for his wife, but inside he's crushed. (Again showing he's nuts about her.)

FIRST COMPLICATION: Jules checks out Ted, the suspected lover, and is overcome with jealous rage. (At this point we suspect this is a story of murderous adultery, which it isn't. We're working up to a surprise.)

SECOND COMPLICATION: Jules confronts Jo Ann. She admits to going dancing with Ted and says they stopped at his motel to get another pair of shoes. She swears her fidelity to Jules. Jules is mollified. He decides to buy Jo Ann the new house she's always wanted, hoping it will keep her happy. He's terrified of losing her.

THIRD COMPLICATION: Jo Ann tells Jules that Ted is bothering her at work, sending her flowers. Jules confronts Ted. There's a shouting match, threats.

FOURTH COMPLICATION: Ted begins following Jo Ann. Jules goes to the police: They tell him they can't do anything unless Ted does something overt. Ted continues to follow Jo Ann.

FIFTH COMPLICATION: Jules hires a private eye to check on Ted's background. The report is that Ted has been twice arrested for sexual battery on women. The private eye says that for $5,000 he will "persuade" Ted to leave town. Jules pays. The private eye vanishes. The police think he's just gone on a bender, but Jules thinks Ted has murdered him.

SIXTH COMPLICATION: Ted and Jules meet in a restaurant and Ted humiliates Jules, swearing that he will have Jo Ann one way or another and that Jules might as well get used to the idea. Jules stews. His friends tell him he has every moral right to kill the man.

SEVENTH COMPLICATION: Jo Ann comes home distressed and rumpled. She says Ted accosted her in a parking lot. Jules, furious, decides to kill Ted.

EIGHTH COMPLICATION: Jules carefully researches the perfect murder. He finds a kind of thrill in the planning of the deed.

NINTH COMPLICATION: Jules kills Ted. It's a bloody act that horrifies Jules.

TENTH COMPLICATION: Jules gets rid of the body.

ELEVENTH COMPLICATION: Jules, shaken, starts to drink heavily.

TWELFTH COMPLICATION: The police come sniffing around. The wily old investigator, Sheriff Molino, suspects

Jules; in fact, he's certain Jules is his man and lets Jules know it. Now Jules frets and can't sleep, his nerves are shot.

THIRTEENTH COMPLICATION: The private eye comes back. He *was* on a bender. The private eye admits that he made up Ted's arrest record in order to get Jules to give him money to get rid of him. Jules falls into abject despair, thinking Ted was not the threat he thought he was.

FOURTEENTH COMPLICATION: Jules's bizarre behavior has Jo Ann on edge. They fight.

FIFTEENTH COMPLICATION: Jules's work suffers. Rumors are spreading that he killed a man and his friends begin to avoid him.

SIXTEENTH COMPLICATION: The police search the house top to bottom looking for clues and take Jules in for questioning. He sweats under the pressure, but admits nothing.

SEVENTEENTH COMPLICATION: Jo Ann can't stand it. People are staring at her, she says. She and Jules have a fight and Jules blurts out that he killed Ted for her. For her!

EIGHTEENTH COMPLICATION: Jules and Jo Ann are living together but they hardly speak. She seems frightened of him, no matter how much he tries to allay her fears.

THE CLIMAX: Jules spies on Jo Ann and finds out she's planning to leave him. He fears she's going to testify against him. On the night she plans her getaway, he kills her.

THE RESOLUTION: The sheriff suspects Jules again, but he can prove nothing. Jules has lost his business, his house, and all of his friends. Most of all, he mourns the loss of his wife. In the last scene, the sheriff stops by to say that he's retiring and moving to Florida and he'd like Jules to confess before he quits. Jules says no. The sheriff says, "Well, it looks like you got away with murder twice." Jules says ironically, "Did I?"

Okay, now we ask the pertinent questions:

- Is the premise proved? Answer: Yes. Obsessive love does lead to loss of love.

- Are there any superfluous complications? Answer: No. It seems like a tight story: no side roads, no digressions, no alleys.

- Are there ironies and surprises? Answer: Yes. The story as a whole is ironic. There are some nice surprises, as when the private eye shows up again.

- Do the characters grow and develop? Answer: Yes. Jules grows from a successful, self-confident businessman into a depressed drunk. From a man in love to a man wallowing in bitterness and regret.

- Is the story worth writing? Answer: Yes.

And that's how writing with a premise works, from getting the germinal idea to proving it with its complications.

THE MULTIPREMISE NOVEL

A damn good novel may have more than one story. It may, as in Leo Tolstoy's *Anna Karenina,* have two stories. There's the Anna story and there's the Levin story. It may, as in *War and Peace,* have more than two stories. There's the story of Pierre's marriage, the story of Pierre going to war, the story of Prince André's mortal wound, and Natasha's story, among others.

In *Crime and Punishment,* there's the story of the crime and the story of the punishment.

In *Gone with the Wind,* there's the story of Scarlett's loss of Tara and the regaining of it, followed by the story of her disastrous marriage to Rhett Butler.

There is much confusion about the concept of premise when a novel has more than one. Every story has a premise. A novel can have more than one story: hence, more than one premise. In a novel with more than one story, the novel itself has no premise. Think of it as being a vessel that contains the stories.

You might want to tell a story, say, of three sisters: one, a nurse; one, an intellectual; one, a prostitute. These three stories have nothing in common except that their protagonists are related. Sisterhood is the vessel. That's good enough.

You might write a story about four patients of the same shrink, or five people who meet at graduate school. The vessel is simply a device that gives the reader a plausible reason for these stories to be published between the covers of the same book.

One way a novel with more than one story can be designed is to put the stories in a series. Each story would have its own premise, even if the stories are all about the same character or characters.

Here's an example: Say you're writing a historical novel about Sir Alec Cuthbertson, a fictional naval hero during the time of Napoleon. You might open your novel with Sir Alec as a midshipman aboard a frigate caught in a typhoon. Frightened witless, Sir Alec hides in the anchor locker while his mates battle the storm. Afterward, Sir Alec betrays a friend to cover his cowardice, his friend is punished, and Sir Alec is given high honors and a promotion. The premise: *Cowardice leads to triumph.*

In the next part of the novel (a new story), Sir Alec falls in love with the beautiful Lady Ashley. Unfortunately, she is betrothed to Lord Nothingham, Sir Alec's stepfather and mentor. Sir Alec figures Lord Nothingham has to be done away with. Sir Alec contrives to have his stepfather accused of cheating at cards, knowing that he would refuse to fight a duel over it, which leads to Lord Nothingham's disgrace. Lady Ashley would never marry a disgraced coward and marries Sir Alec instead. The premise of this story: *Carnal love defeats filial love.*

Sir Alec is called to war in the next story in the series. Here he runs from the sound of the guns into a fog bank, where he fires his cannon to look good and accidentally sinks the English flagship. The premise: *Cowardice leads to disgrace.*

Next we find Sir Alec in prison awaiting execution, full of remorse. What will remorse lead to? Maybe he volunteers for a suicide mission. Let's say he has a loss of courage and doesn't complete his mission and instead betrays his country and surrenders to the French and falls into psychotic despondency. The premise? *Remorse leads to despondency.*

As you can see, the life of Sir Alec is a series of stories, each with its own premise. His life serves as the vessel. The parts of his life that fall between the stories are skipped, such as the three years he spends in prison eating gruel and playing whist with the other prisoners.

In this design, when reading, say, the first story, the reader knows it is about cowardice; when reading the second the reader knows it's about love; and so on. So, you see, even though the cast of characters may remain the same, the stories have different premises.

Another way to design a multipremise novel is to switch back and forth between the stories. As an example, Sir Alec could have a half-brother, the bastard son of Sir Alec's father and a barmaid. Let's call him Rudolf. Rudolf is a brigand. He loathes his half-brother and has promised to cut off his ears should their paths ever cross.

We could design the novel so that we're continually switching back and forth between the two brothers. Then whenever there is a lull in one story, we switch to the other. The episodes could go like this:

THE OPENING SEQUENCE: Sir Alec's tutor, knowing he'll be fired if Sir Alec does not show improvement, teaches Sir Alec to cheat. Sir Alec learns a valuable lesson: Cheating is good.

WE SWITCH TO RUDOLF. He is suspected of having stolen some apples and is told that if he tells the truth he won't be punished. He tells the truth and is punished. Rudolf learns a valuable lesson of quite another sort.

WE SWITCH BACK TO SIR ALEC. He's in love with a scullery maid, who lets him have his way with her. They are caught in an embarrassing situation. She is banished to the prison colony in Australia, and Alec's father warns him to be more discreet in his dalliances.

BACK TO RUDOLF. He sees his mother cheated out of her wages by the owner of the Hog's Breath Tavern. Rudolf and a half-witted friend plan to rob the joint.

BACK TO SIR ALEC. He goes to London for a visit with his father and is told he's in for a big treat—a trip to the finest bordello in London with his dad.

BACK TO RUDOLF. The robbery goes badly. The tavern owner attacks him and Rudolf splits him open with his cutlass. He's on the run now.

BACK TO SIR ALEC. He's returning on the King's Road, half drunk, singing bawdy songs with dear old dad.

BACK TO RUDOLF. He's waiting with his friend along King's Road, on the lookout for a coach to rob. One approaches: They can hear the bawdy songs being sung.

As you can see, the switchback design can be used to compare and contrast two lives. In novels using the switchback design, the stories are usually more or less of equal importance. You can use this design with more than two stories, of course.

Another type of multipremise novel is where the stories are not equal. One is the main story and the other is the *subplot*. Usually, in a novel with a story and a subplot, the subplot has a major impact on the main story.

A subplot can be inserted in one chunk, be presented in sections in a switchback design, or it can be intertwined. An intertwined subplot is the most difficult subplot to handle. In effect, two stories are being told simultaneously, often sharing some of the same incidents. The intertwined subplot almost always involves love of some kind, usually romantic love.

Let's take the example of Joe, the idealistic farmer, and tell the tale of how Joe's idealism is crushed by economic necessity. Let's see what would happen if Joe meets Hannah, the daughter of a neighbor, and Joe falls in love.

Your earlier premise, *Economic necessity destroys idealism,* would no longer apply, because love is involved. The intertwined premise would then be, say, *Economic necessity can't destroy idealism, but love does.*

In our revised story, then, Joe would stand up to the forces of economic necessity and keep on fighting no matter what, but he's fallen in love with Hannah and she's in with the bad guys, so he gives in to keep her love.

Don't like it?

Maybe you want Joe to keep his idealism in the end. Fine. How about *Idealism brought to ruin by economic forces leads to loss of love* as an intertwined premise?

Okay, in this version, our hero sticks to his idealism despite Hannah's pressuring him. He keeps his idealism and loses his love. Let's see how we might prove it:

THE OPENING SITUATION: Joe, in Berkeley, is making an idealistic protest and gets arrested. This is the last straw for his girlfriend, who breaks up with him. (The girlfriend is added to dramatically show him single and in need of a relationship.)

THE INCITING INCIDENT: Joe is told he owns the farm. He determines to make it totally organic, a model of what farming should be.

FIRST COMPLICATION: Joe arrives at the farm and gets to work, ridding it of everything that is not organic. (Up to here, this is a story of idealism.)

THE SECOND COMPLICATION IS THE OPENING OF THE SUBPLOT: While in town to buy some nails, Joe meets Hannah, who works part time in the hardware store. (In this version she's in college studying to be a biochemist.) He asks her for a date and she says yes.

THIRD COMPLICATION: Some nasty bugs attack his sweet potatoes, but he manages to beat them back some natural way, forgetting his date with Hannah. She has heard about the bugs and shows up to help him. They work to the point of exhaustion.

FOURTH COMPLICATION: Joe and Hannah picnic in a meadow on the farm and kiss. (The reader knows this is a love subplot quite apart from the story of idealism.)

FIFTH COMPLICATION: Locusts wipe out Joe's alfalfa, but he's got enough sugar beets in still to make it. (We're back to the story of idealism being tested.)

SIXTH COMPLICATION: Joe misses a bank loan payment. The bank pressures him to use pesticides. He stands up for his principles.

SEVENTH COMPLICATION: On a moonlight hayride (exquisitely romantic) Joe proposes marriage to Hannah and she accepts. (We're back to the subplot.)

THE CLIMAX OF THE MAIN STORY: A new blight is attacking the sugar beets. Organic methods are failing. Joe and Hannah work into the night. In order to save the farm, pesticides must be used. Joe refuses. "It's our future!" cries Hannah, but Joe sticks to his principles. "If you love me, you'll save our farm," she says. Joe chooses idealism. Hannah leaves him. (Climax of the subplot.)

THE RESOLUTION OF THE MAIN STORY: The bank repossesses the farm.

THE RESOLUTION OF THE SUBPLOT: On his way back to the city, Joe stops to see Hannah at the hardware store. She tells him to have a nice life.

As you can see, the intertwined premise, *Idealism brought to ruin by economic forces destroys love,* has been proven.

MASTERING THE TECHNIQUE OF WRITING WITH A PREMISE

Most of the writers in my classes, when first exposed to the idea of writing with a premise in mind, take a look at what they are writing and try to find a premise for it.

Don't do that.

First, see a half dozen movies and try to describe them in terms of their premise. Ask yourself, What is this story about? Then ask, What happens to the characters in the end? That's all there is to it.

Say we both see the classic *The African Queen.* You say the premise is *Vengeance leads to true love and happiness* and I say it's *Answering the call to patriotism leads to victory.* This doesn't mean that one of us is wrong. It is a desire for vengeance that leads Rosie to become suddenly patriotic and in the end Rosie and Charlie, the heroes, do have a victory, but they also end up being in true love and happy. The important thing is the chain of events would be the same. In essence, we'd both be saying the same thing and that's what's important.

You will quickly see that most successful films have a strong premise and the premise will be effectively and economically proved. There will be character development, ironies, and surprises, and the premise will be well worth proving.

Next, see how the story would change with a different premise. Which sequences could be dropped? What would have to be added?

The next step is to start creating stories with a premise in mind. Simply come up with a premise and indicate by mapping out the complications how it is to be proved. Do one or two a day and in a few weeks you'll have writing with a premise in mind mastered.

From then on, you'll be like an Egyptian stonemason with a chisel. You'll have the tool that will help you craft magnificent masterpieces that may last through the ages.

Having mastered premise, you'll then need a strong narrative voice, which, happily, is next on the agenda.

SIX

ON VOICE OR THE "WHO" WHO TELLS THE TALE

WHY THE WHO AIN'T YOU

As you read this book, you no doubt get a strong impression of its author. You are aware, I hope, that this book was not written by a machine. A personality is coming through the writing. You have probably noticed the narrator's sense of humor and strong opinions.

You may believe that the "I" of the narrator and the "I" of the author, James N. Frey, are one. Not so. The "I" of the narrator is not the "I" of James N. Frey. When James N. Frey sits down to write, he takes on a persona and it is this persona that is the "I" of the narrator. It is an idealized projection of James N. Frey, not James N. Frey the real person. The narrator's persona is full of ebullient optimism. The real James N. Frey has days when he's down. Days when he doesn't listen to his own best advice. Days when he feels like throwing up all over his keyboard because the words just won't flow. But the narrator of this book never has moods like that. The narrator of this book is irrepressibly optimistic, upbeat, cheerful, and sure of himself to the point of cockiness.

This does not mean that the real James N. Frey doesn't believe everything in this book. He believes every single word. But just like everyone else, James N. Frey has better days and worse days: He's sometimes cranky, sometimes worried about the national debt, sometimes just can't get his fingers to dance across the keyboard.

The narrator just sails along, always higher than a kite caught in the jet stream.

So even when I, the real James N. Frey, am depressed because my goldfish croaked, I don't let my depression show through the voice of the narrator. I put on my persona and whack away at the keys, a smile on my lips, a twinkle in my eye.

There are other narrative voices in my repertoire of voices I could use.

As an example, when I was a graduate student in English literature I wrote nonfiction with another voice, a scholarly voice. What follows is from a paper I wrote entitled (groan) "Hermeneutics and the Classical Tradition":

> It is the purpose of this paper to compare the approaches to criticism of Alexander Pope and E. D. Hirsch, Jr. Pope, the Augustan, is perhaps the ultimate neoclassical theoretician and practitioner; Hirsch is an American professor of hermeneutics, schooled by and immersed in that twentieth-century German philosophy known as phenomenology. The dichotomies, parallels and points of departure noted below are only suggestive and are not exhaustive. Hopefully, the picture that emerges will support the thesis that the core of Pope's neoclassical theory of criticism survives in Hirsch's hermeneutics: specifically, the concepts of authorial intent, poetry as an act of consciousness, and genre as central to the poet's art. The focus of this discussion will be within the framework of the "poetry as imitation" versus the "poetry as romantic expression" controversy which has been with us since the dawn of literary criticism, and will no doubt be there at its dusk . . .

Note how pompous the narrator sounds. Words like *dichotomies* and *romantic expression* give the paper a scholarly tone. The selectivity of the words and phrases creates the narrative voice. A scholar would never use *damn good*, as an example, just as the breezy, friendly voice of this book would never use a mouthful like *hermeneutics*.

A strong narrative voice creates a feeling in the reader that the writer knows what he or she is talking about. It creates trust. It lets the reader relax the critical faculty and go with the flow of the words. In nonfiction, a strong narrative voice is created by tone and a command of facts. In fiction, a strong narrative voice is created by tone and a command of detail.

Here's an example of a weak narrative voice in nonfiction:

> Living in the San Francisco Bay Area is very pleasant. The weather is good and the air is clean. You can go sailing on the bay year round. There are many fine restaurants and interesting places to go, both for the tourists and the residents.

Because the selected words are generalized, gaseous, and bland, the reader senses that the narrator either doesn't really know his subject or he's mentally incompetent or both. Let's try it with a stronger voice:

> Living in the San Francisco Bay Area is a hoot. You can watch the tourists burn money at Fisherman's Wharf, Pier 39, and boutiques downtown where a ten-dollar hat sells for $99.95. You can watch them pay five bucks for a ten-cent trinket in Chinatown that was probably made in Mexico. The people who live here never go to such places, not when there's a beautiful emerald green bay foaming with whitecaps waiting to be sailed, and all those shadowed hiking trails among the ageless, regal, silent sequoias less than twenty miles north.

This has a lot more life in it—more personality. A phrase like "is a hoot" gives the piece a bit of spice. Specific details of the "emerald green bay foaming with whitecaps" is a concrete image that creates a sense of place. We can see the bay and the boats, feel the regalness of the "silent" sequoias.

Harold was a good worker and a good husband. He dressed well and loved to go hiking on the weekends. His wife liked to go with him, but they usually left the children at home. When they hiked together they loved to talk about the future.

The voice is bland and the details are all gaseous generalities like "good worker," "good husband," and "liked to go hiking." The reader gets the feeling that the person writing this does not have much to say. Here's how it might be strengthened by making the details more concrete and specific:

Harold busted his hump six days a week at Kensington Machine Shop drilling holes in custom-made bathroom fixtures. When not on the job, he dressed as nattily as he could: sharkskin suits, alligator shoes, silk shirts. Sundays, he'd go hiking with his wife, Jewel, and they'd talk about how he was going to bust out one of these days, say *adiós* to the machinist trade and go to Hollywood and become a special-effects man, like his idol William B. Gates III.

Here the narrative voice has personality to it. Expressions like "busted his hump" give some color to the narrative. So does "nattily," which is not only descriptive of the character, but creates the impression that the narrator has a personality.

Here is perhaps a better example of a strong narrative voice in fiction:

Scarlett O'Hara was not beautiful, but men seldom realized it when caught by her charm as the Tarleton twins were. In her face were too sharply blended the delicate features of her mother, a Coast aristocrat of French descent, and the heavy ones of her florid Irish father. But it was an arresting face, pointed of chin, square of jaw. Her eyes were pale green without a touch of hazel, starred with bristly black lashes and slightly tilted at the ends. Above them, her thick black brows slanted upward, cutting a startling oblique line in her magnolia-white skin—that skin so prized by Southern women and so carefully guarded with bonnets, veils, and mittens against hot Georgia suns.

Notice how concrete and specific the details are; this creates the feeling that the voice is sure-footed. The narrator is showing not only what Scarlett looks like, but is also revealing her genetic makeup and the attitudes of Southerners. The voice is impersonal, a reporter's voice, giving no judgments or opinions, but rather stating the facts. But its tone is slightly melodramatic, almost heroic: *an arresting face, pointed of chin, square of jaw,* which is appropriate for the melodramatic story. This is a narrator clearly in control of her material with a lot to say.

Stephen King uses just such a narrator in portions of *Carrie:*

> Momma was a very big woman, and she always wore a hat. Lately her legs had begun to swell, and her feet always seemed on the point of overflowing her shoes. She wore a black cloth coat with a black fur collar. Her eyes were blue and magnified behind rimless bifocals. She always carried a large black satchel purse and in it was her change purse, her billfold (both black), a large King James Bible (also black) with her name stamped on the front in gold, and a stack of tracts secured with a rubber band. The tracts were usually orange, and smearily printed.

The writing here has wonderful details: *her feet always seemed on the point of overflowing her shoes . . . her name stamped on the front with gold.*

You may have heard that good fiction is written with the "author invisible," which means that the narrator can be Godlike, but should not come through, that the voice should be neutral. This is not only a pseudo-rule, it is bad advice, which is very often given to beginning writers. In fact, I gave it myself in *How to Write a Damn Good Novel.* The author (narrator) should not be invisible. Anything but. Macauley and Lanning in *Technique in Fiction* (1987) put it this way: "The narrator as agent has a habit of defying the author's plans and taking on a definite personality of his own. And in the best fiction, so he should." Yes, so he should.

Dostoevsky's narrative voice in *Crime and Punishment* lets the personality of the narrator burst through. Here's how he describes his protagonist, Raskolnikov:

> His clothes were so miserable that anyone else might have scrupled to go out in such rags during the day time. This quarter of the city, *indeed,* was not particular as to dress. In the neighborhood of the Sennaya or Haymarket, in those streets in the heart of St. Petersburg, occupied by the artisan classes, no vagaries in costume call forth the least surprise. Besides the young man's fierce disdain had reached such a pitch, that, notwithstanding his extreme sensitiveness he felt no shame at exhibiting his tattered garments in the street. He would have felt differently had he come across anyone he knew, any of the old friends whom he usually avoided. Yet he stopped short on hearing the attention of a passer-by directed to him by the thick voice of a tipsy man shouting: "Eh, look at the 'German hatter!'" The young man snatched off his hat and began to examine it. It was a high-crowned hat that had originally been bought at Zimmermann's, but had become worn and rusty, was covered with dents and stains, slit and short of a brim, a frightful object in short. Yet its owner, far from feeling his vanity wounded, was suffering rather from anxiety than humiliation.

Although the narrator certainly has Godlike omniscience in that he knows everything about the character and the city, the narrator's personality is shining through in his sympathetic portrayal of his protagonist's feelings: *He felt no shame . . . He would have felt differently had he come across anyone he knew . . . far from feeling his vanity wounded . . .* This novel is being written as if the author knew the man personally and cared deeply for him.

A little later, after the protagonist's first encounter with the woman pawnbroker, Raskolnikov is shocked by his murderous thoughts. He finds them loathsome and disgusting and goes into a filthy bar and has a drink:

> He felt instantly relieved and his brain began to clear. "How absurd I have been!" said he to himself,

"there was really nothing to make me uneasy! It was simply physical!" Yet in spite of this disdainful conclusion, his face brightened as if he had been suddenly relieved from a terrible weight, and he cast a sociable glance around the room . . .

It is the narrator who sees the conclusion he comes to as "disdainful." The narrator, in other words, is given to making judgments on the character, and is hardly "invisible."

Neither is the narrator of *Pride and Prejudice:*

> Mr. Bingley had soon made himself acquainted with all the principal people in the room; he was lively and unreserved, danced every dance, was angry that the ball closed so early, and talked of giving himself one at Netherfield. Such amiable qualities must speak for themselves. What a contrast between him and his friend! Mr. Darcy danced only once with Mrs. Hurst and once with Miss Bingley, declined being introduced to any other lady, and spent the rest of the evening in walking about the room . . .

That *What a contrast between him and his friend!* is the narrator's interpretation of things, giving judgments, editorializing. Invisible? Hardly.

Tom Wolfe's narrator in *The Bonfire of the Vanities* (1987) isn't invisible either:

> . . . Sherman McCoy was kneeling in his front hall trying to put a leash on a dachshund. The floor was a deep green marble, and it went on and on. It led to a five-foot-wide walnut staircase that swept up in a sumptuous curve to the floor above. It was the sort of apartment the mere thought of which ignites flames of greed and covetousness under people all over New York and, for that matter, all over the world. But Sherman burned only with the urge to get out of this fabulous spread of his for thirty minutes.

The tone of course is satiric, but clearly the narrator's personality is shining through, giving you his slant on things: *ignites flames of greed and covetousness.*

Kurt Vonnegut's narrator in *Breakfast of Champions* is not only not invisible—he's downright opinionated:

> This is a tale of a meeting of two lonesome, skinny, fairly old white men on a planet which was dying fast.
>
> One of them was a science-fiction writer named Kilgore Trout. He was a nobody at the time, and he supposed his life was over. He was mistaken. As a consequence of the meeting, he became one of the most beloved and respected human beings in history.
>
> The man he met was an automobile dealer, a *Pontiac* dealer named Dwayne Hoover. Dwayne Hoover was on the brink of going insane.

The narrator who is not invisible can evoke a certain mood of gravity by the use of voice alone. Take Clive Barker's narrator in *Weaveworld:*

> Nothing ever begins.
>
> There is no first moment; no single word or place from which this or any other story springs.
>
> The threads can always be traced back to some earlier tale, and to the tales that preceded that; though as the narrator's voice recedes the connections will seem to grow more tenuous, for each age will want the tale told as if it were of its own making.
>
> Thus the pagan will be sanctified, the tragic become laughable; great lovers will stoop to sentiment, and demons dwindle to clockwork toys . . .

Notice how the narrative voice has created a sense that the story that is about to be told is an ageless one, momentous, mythic.

However, the author as commentator of his own work can go too far. As Macauley and Lanning say in *Technique in Fiction*, "The modern employment of . . . (the author invisible narrator) came from a revulsion against the habit eighteenth- and nineteenth-century writers had of interrupting. It is called an 'authorial intrusion' and it comes when the author in his own person drops in for a chat with the reader."

John Fowles's *The French Lieutenant's Woman*, his deliberate twentieth-century version of a nineteenth-century novel, is illustrative:

> ... Sam, at that moment, was thinking the very opposite; how many things his *de facto* Eve *did* understand. It is difficult to imagine today the enormous difference then separating a lad born in the Seven Dials and a carter's daughter from a remote East Devon village. Their coming together was fraught with almost as many obstacles as if he had been an Eskimo and she, a Zulu. They had barely a common language, so often did they not understand what the other had just said.

It does sound as if the author had stopped by for a chat, doesn't it?

Authorial intrusion can get out of hand. One way is what William C. Knott in *The Craft of Fiction* calls "Author's Big Mouth." Authorial intrusion is overdone when it becomes a commentary on the events or is used as blatant foreshadowing, such as the author giving away what's ahead, like:

> Freddy left, slamming the door behind him, got into his car, and drove off down the road toward what would prove to be the biggest mistake of his life.

This would be a case of the author "shattering the illusion of reality," Knott would say, reminding readers that they're reading "a fabricated product."

THE FIRST VERSUS THIRD PSEUDO-RULE AND OTHER MYTHS

The narrator is a character, and you should think of your narrator as a character whether or not you're writing in the first person. Don't believe the pseudo-rules about what you can do in first versus third person. Virtually *anything* you can do in first person you can do in third and vice versa.

Take Camus's *The Stranger,* which uses the first-person narrator to create what is often called "intimacy." You've no doubt been told this cannot be achieved with a third-person narration. In the following scene, the first-person narrator has arrived at the funeral parlor where his dead mother had been laid out:

> Just then the keeper came up behind me. He'd evidently been running, as he was a little out of breath.
>
> "We put the lid on, but I was told to unscrew it when you came, so that you could see her."
>
> While he was going up to the coffin, I told him not to trouble.
>
> "Eh? What's that?" he exclaimed. "You don't want me to . . . ?"
>
> "No," I said.
>
> He put back the screwdriver in his pocket and stared at me. I realized then that I shouldn't have said, "No," and it made me rather embarrassed. After eyeing me for some moments he asked:
>
> "Why not?" But he didn't sound reproachful, he simply wanted to know.
>
> "Well, really I couldn't say," I answered.
>
> He began twiddling his white mustache, then, without looking at me, said gently:
>
> "I understand."

The narrative is intimate and personal, and nicely done. It evokes the feeling of awkwardness and sadness common to these occasions. Let's see what happens when we change this to third person:

> Just then the keeper came up behind Meursault. The keeper had evidently been running, as he was a little out of breath.
>
> "We put the lid on, but I was told to unscrew it when you came, so that you could see her."
>
> When they were going up to the coffin, Meursault told him not to trouble.

"Eh? What is that?" the keeper exclaimed. "You don't want me to . . . ?"

"No."

The keeper put back the screwdriver in his pocket and stared at Meursault, who realized then that he shouldn't have said, "No," and he felt rather embarrassed. After eyeing Meursault for some moments, the keeper asked:

"Why not?" But he didn't sound reproachful, Meursault thought, he sounded as if he simply wanted to know.

"Well, really I couldn't say," Meursault answered.

The keeper began twiddling his white mustache, then, without looking at Meursault, said gently:

"I understand."

Okay, what "intimacy" is lost? Sorry, but there isn't any intimacy lost. Not an iota. Not a crumb. The third-person version evokes the feeling of awkwardness and sadness just as well as the first-person version.

Let's take a look at another example. We'll start with the supposed less intimate way, with a third-person narrator as Stephen King wrote it in *Carrie:*

He slid across the seat and kissed her, his hands moving heavily on her, from waist to breasts. His breath was redolent of tobacco; there was the smell of Brylcreem and sweat. She broke it at last and stared down at herself, gasping for breath. The sweater was blotted with road grease and dirt now. Twenty-seven-fifty in Jordan Marsh and it was beyond anything but the garbage can. She was intensely, almost painfully excited.

Okay, now for the translation, which, according to the first-person-is-more-intimate theory, should be more intimate:

He slid across the seat and kissed me, his hands moving heavily on me, from waist to breasts. He smelled of tobacco, Brylcreem, and sweat. I broke it at last and stared down at myself, gasping for breath. The sweater was blotted with road grease and dirt now. Twenty-seven-fifty in Jordan Marsh and it was beyond anything but the garbage can. I was intensely, almost painfully excited.

Not too difficult to make the switch. *Redolent* had to go: It wouldn't have been in her vocabulary. Nevertheless, all the same fictional values are being communicated to the reader in either version. There is no gain in intimacy when it is switched to first person.

That's fine, you say, but if the first-person narrator is more colorful, you couldn't switch—you'd lose the color. Okay, let's take a look at some colorful first-person narrative:

> My name is Dale Crowe Junior. I told Kathy Baker, my probation officer, I didn't see where I had done anything wrong. I had gone to the go-go bar to meet a buddy and had one beer, that's all, while I was waiting, minding my own business, and this go-go whore came up to my table and started giving me a private dance that I never asked for.
>
> "They move your knees apart to get in close," I said, "so they can put it right in your face. This one's named Earlene. I told her I wasn't interested. She kept right on doing it, so I got up and left. The go-go whore starts yelling I owe her five bucks and this bouncer comes running over. I give him a shove, was all, go outside, and there's a green-and-white parked by the front door waiting. The bouncer, he tries to get tough then, showing off, so I give him one, popped him good thinking the deputies would see he's the one started it. Shit, they cuff me, throw me in the squad car, won't even hear my side of it. Next thing, they punch me up on this little computer they have? The one deputy goes, 'Oh, well look it here. he's on probation. Hit a police officer.' Well, then they're just waiting for me to give 'em a hard time. And you don't think I wasn't set up?"

Seems as if it would impossible to do that in a third-person narrative without losing its color, doesn't it? But the above is a translation;

that's not the way it was published. The original version is in third person. It's the opening of Elmore Leonard's *Maximum Bob*. Here's the way Elmore Leonard wrote it:

> Dale Crowe Junior told Kathy Baker, his probation officer, he didn't see where he had done anything wrong. He had gone to the go-go bar to meet a buddy of his, had one beer, that's all, while he was waiting, minding his own business and this go-go whore came up to his table and started giving him a private dance he never asked for.
>
> "They move your knees apart and get in close," Dale Crowe said, "so they can put it right in your face. This one's name was Earlene. I told her I wasn't interested, she kept right on doing it, so I got up and left. The go-go whore starts yelling I owe her five bucks and this bouncer come running over. I give him a shove was all, go outside and there's this green-and-white parked by the front door waiting. The bouncer, he tries to get tough then, showing off, so I give him one, popped him good thinking the deputies would see he's the one started it. Shit, they cuff me, throw me in the squad car, won't even hear my side of it. Next thing, they punch me up on this little computer they have? The deputy goes, 'Oh, well look it here. He's on probation. Hit a police officer.' Well, then, they're just waiting for me to give 'em a hard time. And you don't think I wasn't set up?"

Notice that the author used a long quote to get the reader solidly into Crow's speech pattern, but so what? It's a legitimate device. It's just one more way to transmit the intimate fictional values using third person. The trick is, of course, to get the color through the viewpoint of the characters. But even that is not a hard-and-fast rule. In Ken Kesey's *Sailor Song* (1992), as an example, the third-person narrator has no trouble with colorful language:

> Billy the Squid was a disagreeable and pompous little prick, but he made a good president. He had the capacity to pour a lot of creative energy into a project, then back it up with chemicals.

Okay, then, the pseudo-rule that first person is more intimate and colorful than third is just a lot of bunk. The truth is, the same fictional values, intimacy, atmosphere, color, *anything,* can be done equally well in either voice.

Au contraire, you say. It is a well-known fact, you argue, that in a first-person narrative you can't depict scenes in which the first-person narrator is not present. It's an iron-clad rule that first person is much more limited than third.

More bunk.

Beginning writers are always told that you shouldn't choose a first-person narrator because first-person narrators can't show us what is happening out of the character's purview, which is not true. You *can* show scenes that are out of the character's purview. Here's an example of a scene written in third-person omniscient narrative, as Stephen King wrote it:

> The house was completely silent.
> She was gone.
> At night.
> Gone.
> Margaret White walked slowly from her bedroom into the living room. First had come the flow of blood and the filthy fantasies the Devil sent with it. Then this hellish Power the Devil had given to her. It came at the time of the blood and the time of hair on the body, of course. Oh, she knew the Devil's Power. Her own grandmother had it. She had been able to light the fireplace without ever stirring from her rocker by the window . . .

The pseudo-rule says that if this book were written in first person (in Carrie's voice) it would be *impossible* to go into Margaret White's head as is done in the above third-person narrative sample. Let's see if it's true. All it takes is a little sleight of hand. Let's say the novel was narrated in Carrie's first-person voice and she's just left for the prom, where her mother didn't want her to go:

> After I was gone, the house was no doubt completely silent.

I know Mother would linger in her bedroom thinking only one thought: She is gone. At night. Gone.

She'd walk slowly from her bedroom into the living
room, thinking first had come the flow of blood and the
filthy fantasies the Devil had sent me, her daughter. Then
this hellish power the Devil had given me. She'd think it
had come at the time of the blood, the time of hair on
the body, of course. She'd think she knew well the Devil's power. Her own grandmother had had it, and she'd
remember seeing her light the fire in the fireplace without
ever stirring from her rocker by the window . . .

All of the same fictional values, the atmosphere, the intimacy, the
characterization, have been communicated to the reader. You see,
no matter what viewpoint of voice you choose, you have no limits
and are not giving up one damn thing. Except, of course, if the first-
person narrator you've chosen is not capable of good observation
and insights, or colorful language. Or dies before the end of the
story.

The point to all this, of course, is that with whatever viewpoint
and voice you choose, you should exploit the possibilities of the
viewpoint and voice you have chosen rather than feel constrained
by its limitations. Some writers have a better natural feel for one
voice over another, and there are genre considerations as well.
Tough-guy detective novels are often in first person in a tough-guy
voice, while romances are almost always in third person using
flowery, melodramatic language.

THE WRITER PUMPING IRON: DEVELOPING YOUR VOICE

Having a strong voice is as important to you as a writer as knowing
your craft. A strong voice will impress an agent and an editor.

Trying to develop a strong narrative voice, or even the need
for one, is usually beyond a beginning writer's abilities. It's difficult
for a beginning writer to even hear the voice.

The reason for this is simple. Most beginning writers have suffered from being exposed to the typical American education. They

were taught how to write as academics. Once their minds have been put into that straitjacket, they seem unable to free themselves except by the most strenuous effort.

When you would write an essay in fourth grade, or fifth, or seventh, or twelfth, or even in college, the emphasis was always on the grammar, the formal structure, and if any attention was paid at all to the content it was always in the context of whether you had adequately addressed the topic assigned by the teacher.

No one ever said you should have a strong idea. Or that you should use a strong, colorful voice. Your personality was assiduously expunged from the material. If you wrote *gee whiz* in the middle of a term paper, it was struck out with a red pen for being "colloquial" and words such as *interface* were called "jargon." If you expressed a little honest outrage at the stupidness of the assignment to, say, compare and contrast the symbolism of the whale in *Moby Dick* to the *A* in *The Scarlet Letter* you would be flunked.

You were rewarded if you "backed up" what you said with copious quotes. And you were rewarded with high grades if you shared the teacher's point of view and wrote in the most banal, toneless, dead, dull, and lifeless academic style. In other words, each and every essay in the class was judged on how well it matched up to the ideal paper, which was well organized, grammatical, and dead.

I'm ashamed to admit it, but I briefly taught this kind of writing in college and I was told by my supervisor that what was being said didn't matter, particularly. And there was to be no vulgarization, which meant a lot of damn good vocabulary couldn't be used. Now what the hell good is writing anything if what is being said doesn't matter? Or if the personality of the writer is choked off? This attitude on the part of the educational establishment is the reason dull writing abounds and good writing is as rare as an orchid in the Alps.

Since most of us were in deadly fear of taking home a bad report card, we did our damnedest to please our teachers. Most of us started stamping out me-too papers and if we had any misgivings we swallowed them. Usually we asserted our individuality in our papers only in our attempts to do them quickly, so we could brag to our friends that "I gave them what they want, but it only took me three hours to do twenty pages."

But now that you're writing fiction, you must let the lion within you out and let it roar.

To do that, make a close study of authors with a strong narrative voice and see how they achieve it. Copy some of them word for word, then write imitations of them. If you do this daily, you will soon be able to write in half a dozen voices.

Then practice writing the same passages in the different voices.

Here, as an example, is a section of a novel written in what you might call a standard spy-novel style with a neutral voice:

> Biggs arrived at his tiny cubicle in Section Four early that morning and started going through the reports that had come in the night bag from Cairo. Pretty much the same old thing. Requests for more money for Ace Two, who was negotiating with a clerk at the Soviet Consulate for some rocketry technology. A request for a month's leave for the staff cryptologist. Repair requisitions for eavesdropping equipment damaged by the Soviet double agent in the Egyptian defense ministry.
>
> He stamped most of the requests approved and sent them on to his supervisor for final processing. Then he started working on a memo to the station chief in Alexandria about the leaks to the media about the movements of the carrier force off the coast of Syria. His phone rang. It was Hilson's secretary saying he was wanted right away in the deputy director's office for an emergency meeting. He had no idea what the old man wanted, but he felt a tight ball of fear forming in his stomach.

Now let's try the same thing with a different cast to it. Spy thrillers are often written with a cynical tone, which gives the narrative voice an added dimension:

> Biggs arrived at his tiny cubicle in Section Four early that morning and started going through the reports that had come in the night bag from Cairo. The usual fiddle-faddle, Biggs thought. Requests for more money for Ace Two, who was negotiating with the greedy clerk at the Soviet Consulate for rocket technology. A staff cryptologist wanting a month's leave in Majorca, where he'd probably be selling the rocket technology back to the Soviets. Repair requests for the eavesdropping equip-

ment damaged by the Soviet double agent in the Egyptian defense ministry. Such a troublesome lot, those Egyptians, thought Biggs. Change sides as often as they change their socks.

He stamped most of the requests approved and sent them on to his brain-dead supervisor to be rubber stamped. Then he started working on a memo to the station chief in Alexandria concerning those irritating leaks to the media about the movements of the carrier force off the coast of Syria. His phone rang. It was Hilson's cold-voiced secretary saying he was wanted right away in the deputy director's office for an emergency meeting. He had no idea what the old man wanted, but he felt a tight ball of fear forming in his stomach.

The same thing could be written in first person:

I got to my rat hole of a cubicle in Section Four early that morning and started going through the reports that had come in the night bag from Cairo. Same old crap. Ace Two wanted more money to buy the loyalty of that greedy little bastard at the Soviet Consulate, a clerk who had dreams of becoming a Rockefeller by selling his country's rocket secrets. Then there was a request for a month's leave for a staff cryptologist who wanted to go to Majorca, probably to sell his country out to the Bulgarians. And once again there was a repair requisition for the eavesdropping equipment damaged by the Soviet double agent in the Egyptian defense ministry. That guy, soon as I caught him, was going to get ground up and mixed with mud at the bottom of the Nile.

Okay, so I stamped most of the requests approved and sent them on to my supervisor, who would approve them without looking. Then I started working on a memo to the station chief in Alexandria about the goddamn leaks to the media of the movements of our carrier force off the coast of Syria. The phone rang. It was Hilson's secretary: she said I was wanted in the deputy director's office for an emergency meeting. Her voice was frosty. I had no idea what the old man wanted, but for some reason I had this tight little ball of fear forming in my gut.

Working over the same pieces of material like this, using different narrative voices, will help you strengthen your voices and develop new and fresh ones.

It is the narrator, then, who informs the reader, makes the antecedent action (what's happened to the characters before the story began) vivid, gives us the background on the characters, and points the way to the deeper meanings in the story. The attitudes and viewpoints of the narrator are important for establishing the author/reader contract, which will be discussed at length, next, in Chapter Seven.

SEVEN

THE AUTHOR/READER CONTRACT OR DON'T PROMISE A PRIMROSE AND DELIVER A PICKLE

THE BASIC CONTRACT

The notion of a contract is a simple one. It is an exchange of promises. Party A promises something and gets something in return; party B promises something and gets something in return. You buy a house, you promise money, you get a house. The seller promises to give you a house, gets money. Simple.

A real estate contract is a formal contract. A prenuptial agreement is a formal contract. A time-payment plan purchase agreement is a formal contract.

There are informal contracts that are just as binding. These are implied contracts. You make an appointment with your dentist, you agree to be there at the appointed time to suffer the pain, he agrees to be there at the appointed time to inflict it.

When you write a novel you make a contract with the reader. The basic contract with the reader is this: You promise a damn good novel; your reader pays damn good money for it. But there's more to it than that. Much more.

Besides being damn good, your reader expects the novel to be of a general type—either *genre*, *mainstream*, or *literary*.

99

GENRE

Genre novels are sometimes called "category," "pulp," or "trash" novels. They are usually sold as rack-sized paperbacks (though occasionally they're sold in hardback), which fit supermarket or drugstore book racks. When sold in bookstores, they're usually in the back of the store on shelves divided into their various types: mystery, science fiction, fantasy, horror, romance, Gothic, western, political thriller, techno-thriller, historical, male adventure, and so on.

Genre novels are read by people who want a good read, an entertainment. If you're writing one, part of your contract with the reader is that your novel will conform to the conventions of the genre. In the mystery, as an example, there's going to be a murder and someone will solve it, and in the end the murderer will be brought to justice.

Some genres, such as the romance, go beyond simple conventions: They're formulaic. The publishers will even provide a tip sheet for writers that spells out the requirements of the formulas. As an example, the tip sheet might call for the heroine to be twenty-three to twenty-eight with blond or auburn hair, have strong skills in the workforce, but be struggling financially. The specifications might call for the hero to be thirty-two to thirty-eight and rich with dark brown or black hair. Another requirement might be that the couple may have sex only if there's a commitment. The formulas are specific and rigid and if you are writing for this market you must stick to them.

The best way to learn conventions when the publishers do not provide tip sheets is to read a few dozen novels of the type you plan to write. You'll quickly get a sense of the conventions. Spy thrillers, as an example, are usually written in third person, with several viewpoints. They're often set in several locales throughout the world. The spies use exotic spycraft and don't shrink from killing, drugging, kidnapping, and so on. They are usually motivated by what they perceive as their patriotic duty. The protagonists have a surface cynicism, though at heart they are idealists. They are modern-day knights going out to do battle against modern-day dragons. The heroes and heroines are pitted against a great evil, usually a conspiracy on an international scale.

None of these conventions are written in stone, of course.

They are simply conventions, which can be bent or even occasionally broken—unlike formulas, which publishers enforce with maniacal zeal.

In addition to reading a mountain of novels to learn the conventions, you'll find it's a good idea to join organizations such as Mystery Writers of America or Romance Writers of America, and attend some of the workshops and conferences that abound for all types of fiction. There are several journals devoted to the writing of genre fiction. I subscribe to *Mystery Scene,* as an example, which is loaded with information on mystery writing. Almost all of their articles are written by top mystery writers. There are also journals for writers of science fiction, westerns, horror, and others.

Within the major genres are subgenres. There are over a hundred different subgenres of romance novels alone. Mysteries come in different types: tea cozy, hard-boiled, soft-boiled, innocent-at-risk, comic mysteries, and so on. Among the thrillers, there are cartoon-type international thrillers, and there are serious international thrillers. Ian Fleming wrote the cartoon type, while John le Carré writes the serious type. Readers will expect you to stick to the conventions of the subtype as well as to the conventions of the genre as a whole. As an example, in a hard-boiled mystery it is okay for the hero to take personal vengeance upon the villain; in a soft-boiled or a tea cozy, it is not.

MAINSTREAM

The conventions for mainstream novels are not as rigid as they are for genre fiction. Mainstream novels are sold either in hardback or rack-sized paperback. The recently released mainstream novels are usually found in bookstores, usually near the front door, usually in large stacks or in those cardboard display boxes they call kiosks. Mainstream novels often are the ones backed by the publisher with gargantuan promotional budgets.

Mainstream novels are sometimes glitzy melodramas that feature limousines and high living. Glitz novels are usually set in places like Monte Carlo or Buckingham Palace or the Mexican Riviera, and involve characters brimming over with naked ambition.

Mainstream novels may also be about the immigrant experience, such as Howard Fast used to write and Amy Tan writes now. The immigrant experience is about coming to terms with the culture shock of coming to America. Americans love them: These novels let us look at ourselves through others' eyes.

A huge proportion of mainstream novels is called "women's fiction." These novels usually involve stories of marital problems, divorce and adultery, or mother/daughter relationships. Sometimes these novels are marketed as rack-sized paperback originals and may on the surface appear to be genre novels, but they're not. They don't have strong conventions and they don't follow formulas.

Mainstream novels often have more moral ambiguity than genre novels, which tend to be clearly good versus evil stories. In mainstream novels the characters are more fleshed out than they are in genre novels. A mainstream novel about a detective, as an example, might show the detective at home with his wife and kids, and would exploit other conflicts between, say, the detective and his wife, besides the murder investigation that would dominate a genre novel.

Mainstream novels often have a huge cast of characters. The lead characters are usually well educated, often at Ivy League schools. Frequently one of the delights of a mainstream novel is the setting, which is usually in some glamorous industry—high finance, high fashion, photography, and so on. Life in the mainstream is lived in the fast lane—most of the characters have lots of ready cash. Mainstream novels almost always end happily.

Some genre book authors who have "broken through" are considered mainstream. Sue Grafton, Robert B. Parker, Dean Koontz, Tom Clancy, Danielle Steele are all writing genre novels, but they have broken through and are marketed as mainstream.

Sagas and historical novels are sometimes considered genre novels, sometimes mainstream. Genre writers are often advised to write historicals and sagas as a way of breaking into mainstream.

LITERARY

Literary novels, some assume, don't have conventions. Not so. If you're writing a literary novel, you're writing for the cultural elite and they expect, most of all, what's called "fine writing." You can get away with overuse of adverbs and some clumsiness in mainstream and genre novels, but in literary novels, it's a strong convention that the writing is smooth as silk.

Once, stream-of-consciousness novels featuring Faulkneresque prose, novels of existential despair, and other kinds of philosophical novels topped the list of literary novels, but they are no longer in vogue. One popular form of the literary novel at the moment is called "magical realism"; such novels are imitations of the South American fabulists. Low-life novels are still in. The-suburbs-are-screwed-up novel is still around. Novels of the ethnic experience in America are doing well. Metafiction novels are beginning to fade. Metafiction is self-conscious fiction; that is, the author does not try to pretend the story world is real—the illusion is acknowledged.

Literary novel types are much less stable than the others, so you'd better do a little research before you write one to make sure what you intend to write is current. Read the Sunday *New York Times Book Review* and the *New York Review of Books.* They're very up-to-date with what's in and what's out.

Literary novels are marketed in hardback or trade paperback, which are the same size as hardback, but have a soft cover. Many literary novels are published outside of the New York publishing scene. Small presses, regional presses, and university presses are doing a booming business in literary fiction. In fact, there are probably twenty times more literary novels published by houses outside of the New York publishing industry than inside it.

THE CONTRACT BEYOND THE CONVENTIONS

Your reader will try to guess what your premise is right from the beginning, and if you're holding up your end of the contract you will be trying to prove it. As Macauley and Lanning in *Technique in Fiction* put it, "the all-important thing about the first stage of any fiction is that the author makes certain promises there. A successful novel will bear out those promises. The author should be in full command of his conception, not drifting hopefully toward it."

The reader will see, as an example, that the novel is a story about love and something else right from the beginning. In other words, in fulfilling your part of the contract, you'll let your reader in on what the subject of the novel is—at least part of it. It's okay to allow the rest of premise to show itself a little later. While reading, the reader says, "Okay, this is a love story. Now, how will the character's love be tested?" When the reader sees it will be tested with patriotism, the reader has the second part of the premise. Then if the protagonist's lover's family is also an obstacle, the reader will sense this is a story of love overcoming all obstacles, or failing to overcome all obstacles. In either case, the contract has been made: The author is proving a premise and the reader senses it.

Having settled on the major type of story, the next part of the contract has to do with how the story is written. Even though this book is not a novel, I have a contract with my readers. I've promised to give the reader a lot of good information about writing a damn good novel. I've promised to convey this information in a direct, concise, clear manner using a little humor.

There are other provisions of the contract involving the formal aspects of the novel.

Say you've written the first half of your novel in first person, the way Sir Arthur Conan Doyle wrote Sherlock Holmes stories, using a secondary character like Dr. Watson as your narrator. But halfway through your book you may want the reader to know what is going on with the antagonist, Dr. Moriarty. You feel if the reader doesn't know what he's up to, the suspense is dead, and there's no way Sherlock can later figure it out because it's too complicated even for his magnificent brain.

So what do you do? You could use the journal or diary device, which would not break the contract you've made with the reader— but it may not be in Dr. Moriarty's character to keep a diary or a journal, especially since it would certainly incriminate him if it were ever found.

So you decide to go to a third-person narrator for this one section. But this would be most jarring to the reader and would definitely be a violation of the author/reader contract. The reader would feel betrayed.

One way to handle the problem is by changing the formal aspects of the novel. Novels may be split up into chapters, long or short. The chapters themselves may be broken up into sections, each with its own number or subheading. Or the chapters may be grouped into sections or "books" or whatever. Sometimes sections aren't called anything, but simply labeled with roman numerals.

If, say, your scheme is to switch between a first-person narrator and a third-person narrator late in the book, simply call that section "Book II" and make your switch, and your reader will take it in stride. It's a convention in novel writing that when you start a new section you may change the contract.

Another way to handle the same problem would be to have a short section early in the book from Dr. Moriarty's viewpoint in third person, which would establish that feature of the contract. Then when the switch was made again late in the story, it would not be jarring to the reader.

Stephen King divides *Carrie* into two formal sections, Part One and Part Two. Part One he calls "Blood Sport," and Part Two he calls "Prom Night," though he does not change the contract in the second part. He opens "Blood Sport" with a newspaper article describing how a shower of stones fell on Carrie's house out of the sky, then introduces a third-person omniscient narrator, who tells us the meaning of the rain of stones. We quickly come to see that the third-person narration will be mostly in Carrie's viewpoint, but that the author has reserved the right to go into other viewpoints as he wishes. The third-person narration is interrupted with sections from other books written after the incident. These book sections are set off from the narration.

> From *The Shadow Exploded: Documented Facts and Specific Conclusions Derived from the Case of Carietta White,* by David R. Congress (Tulane University Press: 1981) p. 34:
>
> It can hardly be disputed that failure to note specific instances of telekinesis during the White girl's earlier years must be attributed to the conclusion offered by White and Sterns in their paper *Telekinesis: A Wild Talent Revisited*—that the ability to move objects . . .

The other books quoted are *Ogilvie's Dictionary of Psychic Phenomena* and *My Name is Susan Snell,* along with parts of supposed articles from magazines such as *Esquire* and *Science Yearbook.*

Right from the beginning, the author has shown the reader

what kind of book it is and how it will be told and he sticks to it right to the very end.

Gone with the Wind is written in sixty-two chapters, divided into five parts, all written in third-person omniscient viewpoint—mostly, but not exclusively, from Scarlett's viewpoint. But it's clear right from the beginning that this is Scarlett's story, told in lush, melodramatic prose at a fast pace. The contract is made and stuck to throughout the book.

If in the middle of it, say, there was a psychic incident, the contract would be broken. This is not that kind of book. Or if there were a long meditation on the meaning of life or if suddenly the narrative switched on page 482 to Rhett Butler fighting a battle at sea, or if the situation became suddenly Kafkaesque, absurdist, or comical, the contract would be broken. What Margaret Mitchell promises, Margaret Mitchell delivers.

Kafka is Kafkaesque throughout. In *The Trial,* he is Kafkaesque right from the start, which is the contract Kafka makes with the reader. Strange things are happening right away: There's a strange man in K.'s bedroom right on the first page. And the very fact that the protagonist has no name, but is merely called K., is strange in itself. *The Trial* is written in a third-person, limited omniscient viewpoint. The narrator is limited in the sense that the narrator knows what is going on with K., but not what is going on with the law behind the scenes. That would spoil the impact, of course, because the very point of the story is that what goes on with the law is unknowable. It is written in a brusque, no-nonsense style befitting the strangeness of the story. Kafka keeps his contract with the reader till the very end. Formally, the book is divided into chapters with a separate title for each, as if a different aspect of K.'s life is being examined in each one.

Stephen Crane in *The Red Badge of Courage* uses objective viewpoint or distant third person, except when in the viewpoint of the protagonist. Then he uses close third person. Fyodor Dostoevsky in *Crime and Punishment* uses omniscient third person and a "telling" along with "showing" style throughout, which is appropriate to the moral lesson he is teaching. In all of the works that have been used as models in this book, the tone, style, viewpoint, and narrative attitude are preserved beginning to end.

All the novels used as examples in this book have been written in the voice of a "reliable" narrator. The contract with the reader is that all events are set down as they happened and that the author is playing fair with the facts of the situation.

The narrator of a story, by the very nature of the storytellers' art, must withhold things from the reader. In the standard contract, the narrator, who knows the ending of the story, as an example, does not reveal it, but rather tells the story linearly, so that it seems to be unfolding before the reader's eyes. The narrator tells all that's necessary for the reader to know of the events that have already happened, but holds back what is going to happen.

In the standard contract it is a terrible violation to not play fair with the reader. A writer may sometimes get away with it, however, especially if it is done only once. As an example, a science fiction story might open with the first-person narrator talking about a beautiful woman the narrator is hoping to seduce, and not let the reader know that the narrator is a lizard until later.

If such a device at the beginning of the story is used as a kind of hook, okay, but if you try to pull it off more than once, the reader is apt to feel the contract has been violated and close the book.

You can, however, make a contract with the reader that states that the narrator is completely unreliable and it is up to the reader to figure out what is really happening. One example of this is Faulkner's famous retarded narrator, Benjy, watching a golf game in *The Sound and the Fury*. The enjoyment of reading it is getting the sense of what it's like to be in the head of a retarded person. We enjoy it, even though we know that what is being reported is unreliable.

A narrator does not have to be retarded or insane to be unreliable. A narrator might just be highly prejudicial:

> Really, I didn't mind when the Fresians moved in next door. Honest, some of my best friends are Fresians. In fact, when they moved in, I went over and said hi and asked them not to park in front of my house, because I have friends come sometimes and they like to park there. I didn't insist on it, though, but I could tell they didn't like it. Fresians are touchy.

They complained the very first week about my kid throwing apples in their back yard. Why not make an apple pie, I told them, kidding. But you can't kid with a Fresian, no sense of humor . . .

Even though the narrator is unreliable and is giving highly prejudicial testimony, the reader gets the true picture. This is not a violation of the author/reader contract, because the narrator has been unreliable all along. Even if the reader does not catch on immediately, there is no contract violation unless the author doesn't let the reader know the narrator is unreliable until the very end and is playing a sort of joke on the reader. Readers don't like those kinds of jokes. They will send you nasty letters if you do things like that.

PLAYING FAIR

Your part of the contract with the reader obligates you to play fair with the reader. What this means is if, say, you're writing a mystery, you will give the reader a fair chance to outguess the detective; it means that all the facts, clues, and so on will be offered to the reader.

If you're writing a romance—and as we all know, it's part of the fun to keep the lovers apart—you will not keep the lovers apart except through very well motivated circumstances. If they have a misunderstanding, it should be a rational one.

You will keep your contract only by creating a story with absolute verisimilitude. You will do your homework, and you will not, as was done in this book, relate a story of a farmer without doing the research necessary to create a farm scenario.

You will not cheat on suspense by using cheap devices such as the "idiot in the attic" motif (named for the stupid heroines in fifties horror movies who insisted against all common sense on investigating those strange noises in the attics of spooky old mansions). If you're going to write a damn good novel, you'll have to keep your characters at maximum capacity at all times—which means they will not act stupidly or capriciously unless they're drugged, drunk, brain injured, or it is part of their character and is being played for comedy.

The same goes for coincidences and contrivances. You can

have a coincidence if it's played for comedy or if it's the trigger that gets the story started, but after that, it's a violation of your contract. A contrivance is when you have a character who is, say, broke, finding the $100 his aunt sent him for Christmas six years ago in an old shoe. A contrivance is the author solving the characters' problems for them. Avoid contrivances at all cost.

One of the major clauses of the contract states that you will give your characters challenges and they will meet them with their own resources and will develop as a result. You are playing both sides of the game. It isn't enough that you create interesting characters—you have to create interesting obstacles for them to overcome in interesting ways.

Which brings us to one of the biggest violations of the contract: clichés. When a reader buys a novel, it is with the understanding that the material included is new. Not recycled. No cliché stories, no cliché characters, no cliché language. Of course, no writer can keep this part of the contract completely, but as part of your contract you must swear a blood oath to try your damnedest to jettison the clichés before your damn good novel gets published.

You will also swear an oath to avoid bad melodrama.

Bad melodrama is not the same thing as good melodrama. In good melodrama, the characters are well motivated and the situations are reasonably true to life. In bad melodrama, characters act at the behest of the author rather than out of their own, believable, inner needs. There's no good reason, as an example, for Snidely Whiplash to tie poor Pauline to railroad tracks. He does it simply because the author wants him to.

In any good story you're building through a series of minor climaxes to a grand climax and resolution, the ending, where readers are cheated the most often by lazy writers who don't bother to exploit their material dramatically.

Beginning writers have a habit of doing this. They promise a showdown between the protagonist and antagonist, but it never comes off and the story just evaporates in the end. This is the most common and serious violation of the author/reader contract. You've promised a good climax and resolution to the story and you damn well better deliver it. That's your end of the contract.

Okay, you can make the reader dream the fictive dream, you can make your novel suspenseful and people it with interesting characters, and you know how to construct a story with a strong premise and keep your contract with your reader. You're ready to write your damn good novel, so you might as well get started.

But wait!

Before you begin, you've got to be careful not to commit one of the seven deadly mistakes. And what might they be? you ask. They're the subject of the next chapter, of course.

EIGHT

THE SEVEN DEADLY MISTAKES

1. TIMIDITY

A writer of fiction," Edwin A. Peeples says in *A Professional Storywriter's Handbook* (1960), is someone who "hurls himself against all odds . . . seizing today's exultation or catastrophe and the experience of history, we attempt to forge them into a tale that excites, amuses, instructs, and moves. The work is no career for the timid."

Growing up, I'd always considered myself a brave fellow.

I used to go skiing with a couple of lunatics (whom my father called "bad companions") and we'd shush through a woods, sometimes on trails covered with ice, sometimes at night when you couldn't see the next turn, the next dip in the trail, the next bare spot that could send you flying ass over teakettle. And often did.

In the summer I'd water-ski, standing on somebody's shoulders, right off the lake and up onto the grass in the front yard of our summer home. I'd try anything. Play sandlot tackle football without pads or helmets. Get in fights with my sister, who was a regular Tarzan.

After high school I worked on submarines under construction. You could get burned up, you could get stuff dropped on your head, you could suffocate in a holding tank. I never gave it a thought. What the hell.

When I joined a creative writing workshop for the first time, I was already married and had two kids. By then I was working as an insurance claims adjuster, getting screamed at all day, threatened, occasionally attacked by an irate claimant. But, hey, I had a tough hide, didn't bother me a bit.

But when I'd have to read a five-page short story in my creative-writing workshop, my throat would close up, my mouth would go dry, and I'd tremble all over. Then, while my story was being discussed by the other members of my workshop, I'd feel my stomach tighten up, sweat rolling down my back, my skin turning cold, and little speckles would dance on the insides of my eyelids. Our leader did not, let us say, pull his punches, and each one knocked me a little silly.

I'll give you a small example, a written critique I received once from a workshop instructor:

> Dear Mr. Frey:
> While I find that this piece of work resembles fiction in that it is constructed of words formed into sentences and is imaginative rather than factual, the only other thing it has in common with a story, as far as I can see, is that it has a beginning and an end. There the resemblance stops. What I want to know first is what's the point of this? So Henry's mother-in-law comes back from the dead and takes up where she left off in her campaign to straighten him up. What impact does it have on him? Why does he do *nothing* in the whole seventy-five hundred belabored words of this ?????? but lie there and tremble? And why has the mother-in-law bothered to come back? You seem to think, Mr. Frey, that just because you have found what might be an interesting situation full of dark horrors and mysterious happenings you've somehow created a story. You haven't. I know nothing more of Henry after reading this whole dreary piece than I did after his first yelp when the old gal filters in through the wall . . .

You get the idea. When you're on the receiving end of that kind of criticism, it's painful. Even the bravest turn to putty.

One member of that workshop later told me that she'd often

go to the bathroom and throw up when it was all over with. She's now an award-winning playwright and has sold dozens of short stories to major markets.

Another stormed out, but came back a year later and has since sold a couple dozen novels. Still another said that he never once had a story read in any workshop when he didn't feel as if he was going to pee his pants. He later sold a few novels and made a mountain of moola selling story ideas to TV.

To learn the principles, you have to suffer a little. If the criticism in a workshop is any good, this is the way it is. Your ego is filleted right before your eyes.

It's no wonder that many can't take it. The drop-out rate in a hard-nosed creative writing workshop is often 70 or 80 percent. Why? Because receiving criticism is often painful. It's hard to read something to a group of fellow writers and then listen to them tell you that your prose is limp or muddled or your characters are flat. But it's really the only way to learn.

Timid writers usually end up going from workshop to workshop hoping to find a leader who's not too hard on them. They can't overcome their timidity in the face of honest criticism, so they search out criticism they can take. And they find it. They find it in a "puff" group, where the criticism is soft and infrequent and the praise is profuse. This will doom them.

So what's the solution? It takes guts to be a writer. You've got to overcome your timidity and face up to a solid writers' group. One way to do that is to tough it out. Go to an honest workshop, read one of your stories every chance you get, and just sit there and take it. Soon you will learn that the workshop is discussing your construction, not you, or your ego. Your story is simply a work in progress that you need feedback on to learn how to make it more powerful and effective. If you hang in there, you will learn to cope.

One thing that may help is to learn to joke about it. Another thing is never to get into a discussion about why you wrote it the way you did. If asked, just say something like "I was possessed by the spirit of Annabel Lee," or say you'd prefer the story speak for itself. Never, ever defend or explain your work. Never, ever argue with or disagree with the criticism you receive. Since you asked for it, you've no right to complain. If you don't like it, you can just ignore it. It's your story—you can do what you want with it.

Eventually, as your skills improve, the criticism will get less harsh. There won't be much anyone will have to say except, "Wow!"

A writer can't be timid in his or her work, either.

A writer can't back away from what is strongly dramatic just because the fictional materials may offend someone or produce a lot of tension in the writer during the act of creation. A timid writer is reluctant to put characters to the test.

This often happens when writers attempt to create art from their own situations, trying to solve their problems through the lives of their characters. What usually results is that the characters become frozen, refusing to act. They suffer the same kind of paralysis human beings often experience when trying to solve problems. Makes for pretty bad storytelling.

Another kind of timidity in writing is a reluctance to take risks.

I write thrillers and mysteries. Occasionally I'll come to a place where a villainous character I've created has a sympathetic character just where he wants him, and know what? He's going to do dirty and dastardly things to him. It always amazes me how many of my fellow practitioners tell me I'm making a big mistake, that the readers will rebel against, say, having the protagonist's sidekick cruelly treated, mutilated, or murdered.

Hitchcock did not pull back from having Janet Leigh hacked to death in the shower. If he had, what would have happened to *Psycho*?

Stephen King never pulls back.

And I'm not just talking about being grisly. Did the heroine have to die at the end of *A Farewell to Arms*? Did the hero have to die at the end of *For Whom the Bell Tolls*? No, of course not, but if you want to make an emotional impact on your reader you must produce tragic situations. Tragic, or gory, or horrific, or whatever. You can't pull back. You can't be timid if you aspire to be a damn good novelist.

Don't be timid about trying to achieve new effects.

As an example, say you are embarrassed about writing sex scenes. You might be tempted to write something like this:

> She looked into his deep blue eyes and kissed him
> full on the mouth, feeling the kiss reverberate down to
> the tips of her toes. He drew back for a moment and,

114

turning his head to the side, said, "You impetuous thing, you. Are you sure? Have you thought of what might happen should your husband come home?"

"My husband's coming home Saturday. Until then, I'm yours. All yours. One hundred percent yours."

"Then let's turn off the lights," he said, reaching for the switch . . .

At eight the next morning, she woke to find Mortimer had gone.

This is a sort of truncated version of what might have been a pretty sexy scene.

Often a timid writer runs away from what's tough by going into a flashback. Flashbacks are nice, comfy, warm places where the conflicts and tensions in the "now" of the story have not happened yet, so the writer can retreat there easily to get out of the storm. Running away from conflict is a common course for the timid writer.

Often, novelists are afraid of their emotions. If you have felt, say, an enormous embarrassment in your life at one time and now you are writing a scene in which your protagonist is about to face an embarrassing situation, you may begin to recall your own embarrassment as you write it. This is a good time to explore this fully, to get it all down on paper, no matter how painful it is.

Okay, easily said, you say, but not easily done.

No, it isn't. But if you want to be a damn good novelist you'll learn to do it.

The first step in overcoming timidity is to learn to realize when you're guilty of it, and to immediately take corrective measures. Sometimes simply asking yourself whether you might be running away from conflict is enough to make yourself turn around and face whatever you were running away from.

Writers run away not only from conflict. They also run away from editors and agents.

Soon after I'd completed my first novel, I received this advice:

Go to the bookstore. Find some books similar to yours. Jot down the publishers of these books. Go home and call the publishers and ask for the editorial department. Tell them you want to speak to the editors of the books similar to yours. When the editor comes on the line, tell her or him how much you admire the book. Say that you have written one like it and ask whether they would take a look. Nine times out of ten they'll say yes.

I was horrified. What—call the Olympian gods? On the telephone? Me? James N.—for Nobody—Frey?

It was only later, after having attended a slew of writers' conferences and having met a lot of New York agents and editors, that it began to dawn on me that the reason editors are editors and agents are agents is that most of them are failed writers who haven't the guts to face the blank page and the rejection slip.

They do not have any magic ability. In fact, most of them are work-by-the-numbers kind of people. They put on their pants or pantyhose one leg at a time. If you call them, they will not send hot lightning bolts over the phone lines to turn you into cinders.

In fact, they will respect you for your boldness. They know if a writer believes in himself or herself, chances are the writer is at least a sure-footed one.

While you're at the bookstore, by the way, it might be a good idea to look through the stacks of new arrivals for the bad books that got past the Olympian gods. You'll be amazed to find that half the books are not only bad, but almost unreadable.

Recently *Publishers Weekly,* the number one magazine of the book trade, said that 30 percent of the hardcover books produced in the United States go *directly* from the printer to the remainder house. Thirty percent of the books listed in publishers' catalogs do not get enough orders from book buyers to justify keeping the book in the publisher's warehouse. A remainder house buys these books for pennies, then sells them either through catalogs or to supermarkets or places like Woolworth that market them for a fraction of the fifteen to twenty dollars or more they would have retailed for.

Most of these books are handled by an agent, submitted to an editor, purchased, edited, rewritten, copyedited, proofed, and all that. They have nice, often expensive covers and are listed in the publisher's catalog, but for some reason when the salesmen go to the book buyers, there is no interest in these books.

In other words, editors completely goof it 30 percent of the time. They are just people, and they have no crystal ball. Every book they buy is a guess and a gamble. They might as well guess on yours and gamble with it as with anyone else's. They won't even read it, though, unless someone gives them a sell job.

To get an agent to read your manuscript, you will have to give the agent a sell job. If agents scare you to the point that you can't get up the nerve to give them a sell job, your writing career will go nowhere.

There's another kind of writer's timidity. It has to do with promotion.

I've never met a writer who really likes to promote. Writers often like to sit in the cool of their cubbyholes and plunk away at a keyboard, lost in a la-la land of their imagination. They are often painfully introverted, if not out-and-out hermits. The very idea of being behind the microphone of a radio talk show or in front of a TV camera turns their backbones to piddle. But unfortunately in these times a writer must be a self-promoter or be doomed to obscurity.

How does one get over this dreadful fear of being in the public eye?

According to psychologists, the fear of speaking in public ranks higher than the fear of death. How, then, if you're going to get over this obstacle, do you go about it?

Take a traditional public speaking course. That's probably the quickest way. Dale Carnegie courses are available almost everywhere. Evening courses at high schools and colleges can often do the job cheaper. Toastmaster organizations, found in most major cities, have been effective at teaching public speaking.

Another way is to take acting lessons. It's not only effective, but fun, and will help your writing. If these opportunities are not open to you where you live, I suggest you volunteer as a speaker someplace: a church or a school or a public service group.

So much for the first deadly mistake.

2. TRYING TO BE LITERARY

I've had all kinds of fledgling writers come into my workshops, from near illiterates to near geniuses, from porno writers with their heads in the mud to sci-fi writers with their heads in cloud 2009. I've had mainstream novelists after the big bucks and wide-eyed poets writing narrative you can hum in the shower. I've been impressed and inspired by many, learned from many, and been fired up by some. All except the literati.

Literati are new writers who barely know their way to the keyboard and who are trying to out-James-Joyce James Joyce or out-Virginia-Woolf Virginia Woolf. Though I've had dozens that tried, I've never known one that succeeded.

The problem with literati is this: Instead of attempting to master the principles of creative writing, instead of learning how to make their literary creations fresh and dramatic, literati choose a literary giant as a god and seek to emulate him or her—while all the time claiming to be on the cutting edge of the avant garde because the giant they've selected is way out there.

If in the workshop it is pointed out, say, that his story has no rising action, that it's static, or dull, or slow, the literatus will smile a wry, superior smile and tell you that you obviously haven't read "The Mud at the Edge of Time," the groundbreaking story written by the literary giant whose coattails he's riding to immortality. It's a groundbreaking story because it doesn't bother to show a character's motivation, or it moves by chance instead of by events caused by other events, or it has no ending or no beginning, or every character in the story is a scumbag that repels the reader.

It usually doesn't do any good, but I try to point out a few obvious facts about the imitative work. For one thing, the hugely successful literary giant the literatus is imitating can get any damn thing he or she writes published, and certain critics are poised to praise it no matter what it is, and others are too timid to take on a giant, who everyone knows is a genius with a capital G. Both the critic who praises the giant and those who know better would roast a new writer who committed the same felonies. Telling beginning literati that they can't break the same rules as the rule-breaking giants they're imitating is like trying to explain to four-year-olds why they can't have a martini.

The biggest problem of imitative work is that no one likes an imitator.

If you are going to be one of the literati, pleeeeeeze, first become a great storyteller who uses the principles of dramatic fiction to create masterpieces of craft before you attempt to break the rules. Yes, the rules may be broken successfully, but for every ten or twenty thousand who try only a handful are successful.

Now that I've thrown my thunderbolts at the literati, let me confess that I have committed this very mistake.

My first attempt at novel writing was a fictionalized version of a memoir written by a White Russian soldier about his adventures in the Russian Revolution. Thinking my genius would get me through, I was mucking up the narrative all over the place. I didn't even bother to get the details right. If I didn't know something I should have known, say about the ranks of the officer corps in the Red Army, I just made it up. I switched viewpoint whenever I damned well pleased and generally cheated the reader at every turn—had long dream sequences, flashbacks just for the fun of it.

It didn't publish.

Another literary novel I attempted a few years after that was to be my great autobiographical work. That's the one I called *The Cockroach*. My genius, I thought, was ripening and I was ready to knock the literary world over with it. I did pretty much the same thing, only this time I was surreal. Death played footsie with my hero throughout the story.

I spent, all told, perhaps four years on this tome, envisioning it as the Great American Novel, trying to be literary instead of trying to be damn good.

3 . EGO-WRITING

At a workshop I once attended in Berkeley a young writer read a touching story about a man whose wife of nine years up and left him one day, right out of the blue.

The story opened the moment *after* the wife left, as she slammed the door on the way out. First the man wept, then he drank, then he got together with friends and tried to put his life back together. It ended with the man going out on a date a few weeks after the divorce with his former wife's sister, reconciled to the loss of his wife, hopeful that there is life after a marital breakup.

The writer had a lot of talent: The story showed a lot of insight, was charged with emotion, and the prose was clean and crisp.

During the critical discussion of the story, members of the workshop pointed out that since the reader never saw the wife, there was no *objective correlative* for the man's grief. *Objective correlative* is a technical term coined by T. S. Eliot to describe the necessity for the reader to see and experience the action that evokes an emotional reaction in a story. In other words, if a character is mad because he was insulted, the writer should describe the incident in which the character is insulted. In the case of this story, since we never see the protagonist's wife, we can't identify with his feelings of loss. Perhaps if we had met her and had seen her interacting with the protagonist we would have been able to feel his grief. The way the author had written it, we could feel sorry for the character because he was grieving, but we could not feel the grief itself. We urged the author to begin the story a little earlier in the lives of these characters for that purpose.

The author was not in the least receptive to this criticism.

She thought those of us who agreed with it did not understand what her authorial intent was in this story, and in fact we were looking at the act of creating backward. You see, she said, she was writing not about the relationship, but about *grief,* and was presenting the actions, thoughts, and feelings of the character in a truthful way to the best of her ability. She said she had documented exactly how he overcame his grief, which was what she wanted to do, and that was what she did. It was our job as readers to accept what she had written on its own terms. She was not interested in the least, she said, in "hooking her reader" or enticing him or her into the story world, in creating emotional touchstones to connect the reader to the story, or in getting the reader to identify with her characters or their problems. In other words, she was creating something complete and true to its theme (which interested her), and if it didn't interest the reader, well, too bad for the reader.

This author held to the *author is sovereign* view of fiction writing. She was an ego-writer, of the reader-be-damned school of fiction. In the fifteen years since this incident occurred I've encountered hundreds of adherents to the reader-be-damned school.

You might wonder how you can be a writer if your ego isn't in your writing. Aren't all damn good novelists egomaniacs of some kind?

Well, yeah, of course they are. But the ones who succeed are writing for readers. Let's call them reader-writers, to distinguish them from ego-writers. To be a fiction writer, you have to, as Trollope said, "lay your own identity aside."

At a recent California Writers Club conference, I met an extraordinary writer in her eighties. She was white-haired, wore thick-rimmed glasses, and flashed a big-yellow-toothed grin. She told me she'd started writing when she was thirty-five. She'd always had the itch, she said, and then one fine day her beer-truck driving husband left her with four kids, the bills unpaid, and nothing but air in the refrigerator.

She figured she could make it as a fry cook or a housekeeper, but she had an infected big toe that kept her off her feet. Her neighbor had a typewriter. She borrowed it and started knocking out confession stories.

In her career she had sold, she said, 415 confession stories, 250 others to "everyone from *Cosmo* on down," and 41 novels. At the moment she had four books under contract, three paperback original romances and a hardcover book on gardening.

I asked her what her secret of success was. She said it was simple enough. "When I write, I think of my reader sitting in an easy chair, bone weary after a hard day's work. My job is to make sure she stays in that chair until the book is done, and to do that I write as strong as I can, using every trick I know."

This is how a reader-writer thinks. Please your reader, not your ego.

4. FAILURE TO LEARN TO RE-DREAM THE DREAM

When I started teaching creative writing, I thought if I was lucky I'd have perhaps two or three students with potential in a class of twenty. What I found was the opposite. Almost all of my students were loaded with potential.

What I mean by "potential" is this: They have the ability to create characters a reader can believe in, the power to evoke a scene, a good sense of humor, and a flair for colorful language.

But not all of them had it.

The first time I taught at the University of California Extension, a young woman came into my workshop who had, I thought, very little potential. She was planning to write a series of novels about her suburban family, their petty bickerings, their divorces, diseases, and financial troubles. It was all hopelessly dull and dreary.

She was making all the usual mistakes, and even some not so usual ones, with her story. Flat characters, cliché situations, trite dialogue. Her prose style was clumsy to boot, ungrammatical, and often muddled.

The opening of her novel was a description of a woman bored out of her mind with housecleaning. She offered us thirty pages of dusting. The reader became as bored as the housewife. The workshop was brutal with its criticism.

The next time she submitted her work to the workshop she had managed to take out a little of the dull and put in a little more excitement, but her so-called story still resembled a plate of goulash, a mishmash of events and characters that never went anywhere.

I was dismayed when she signed up for a second semester, and I was tempted to tell her to try the photography class across the hall, because the writing game was obviously not for her. But it has always been my policy to let students decide matters like that on their own. My job is to criticize their manuscripts, not give them advice on what to do with their lives.

The second time she took the workshop, her work improved marginally. The other students and I hammered her with criticism, which she took stoically, even though I could tell she was hurting.

She came back again for another session the next quarter, and the next. After four years and several dozen rewrites she finished her novel. She had taken her characters about as far as she could. She sent the manuscript around to agents and scored a well-known New York agent, much to my amazement. The agent gave it a pretty good shot, but she couldn't place the manuscript and subsequently sent it back.

By that time, she was nearly finished with her second novel, which, in my opinion—and the opinion of most of the members of the workshop—is a smash. It's about a young woman in search of her mother who abandoned her when she was five. It's mysterious, warm, touching, and funny. She still needs help with her grammar, but in every other way she's writing like a pro.

Another young woman was also a member of that first workshop I held at U.C. Extension. June had a doctorate in anthropology and was writing a novel about Indians in Peru. I thought of her as having a lot of potential. Her story generated a lot of enthusiasm in the workshop and I thought she would publish within a year or two. It's been several years now, and not very much progress has been made, even though she's mastered the rules of writing fiction and is a pretty fair critic of others' work.

It was in observing these two women and how they approached rewriting that I discovered what was wrong with many of the talented students I'd been teaching who had not achieved their potential. When I asked the successful young woman about her work, she said that upon entering my class she quickly realized that her ambition was far greater than her abilities, and that if she was ever going to write anything worth reading, she would have to learn how to "re-dream the dream."

What she meant by that, she said, was that when she first sat down to write something, she saw it in her mind. And then she wrote it. After she had a lot of people read it and tell her where it failed, she sat down and re-dreamed the dream. In other words, she could see the story unfold in her mind differently than she had the first time she wrote it.

When I asked the other woman about how she approached her work, she thought a while and said that once she saw a scene a certain way, that was it. It was like a memory. How can you change a memory? It's fixed.

I then realized that an inability to re-dream the dream was the very reason I had taken so long to write something worth publishing. I would write a story, bring it to my workshop, have it criticized, and when it came to reworking it, I was not able to re-dream the dream. I would instead replace the dream with a new dream. I was not rewriting—I was throwing out what I had written and starting all over again.

How do you re-dream the dream? It takes hard work and practice. I suggest to my students that when they sit down to rewrite they start the scene earlier and give the characters different objectives in the scene. In other words, have them want something they didn't want the first time it was written. This will start the scene in a new direction.

Even though re-dreaming the dream is a difficult skill to master, it's a deadly mistake not to learn to do it.

The writers who make this mistake must number in the millions.

A typical case goes like this: The young writer starts out fired by ambition and a sense of mission and purpose. Every young writer feels that he or she has a great untapped talent bursting to get out, and that with a little effort that talent is sure to be recognized. So let's call our typical young writer Heidi Smith.

So what happens to Heidi, who at twenty is fired up by her ambition and sense of mission and purpose?

Okay, first she writes a little short story and submits it to a literary magazine. Gets a printed rejection. Tries a few others. More printed rejections: *Sorry, but not quite right for us.—The Editors.*

She writes a couple more short stories. Gets rejected again. Heidi can't figure it out. She knows she's got talent. She feels her fire. She's worked hard on these stories. How come the rejections?

To find out the answer, she decides to take a short-story writing course. She writes a few more stories, gets some encouragement from her instructor and fellow students. Finds out what she was doing "wrong." Not enough character development. So in goes some more character development. Too much introspection. Cut the introspection. Sort of like fiddling with a cake recipe until it comes out right. Sweeten it up. More sugar. More shortening. A couple more eggs and it'll be just right.

Soon Heidi has a pile of short stories in various stages of development. Her creative writing teacher is high on one or two. They make the rounds of the lit mags. *The Atlantic, The New Yorker, The Swanee Review.* More rejection.

But then something happens that's practically a miracle. Instead of the regular printed rejection form signed "The Editors," Heidi begins to get a personal note scribbled on the rejection form: *Try us again.*

Encouraged, she cranks out a few more stories. Reads some more creative-writing books. Takes some more classes. Polishes the stories until they gleam. Starts submitting again. More rejections. The young writer is now through college. Maybe twenty-four, twenty-five years old. Been writing for four or five years and has not gotten a single thing published, except for perhaps a small poem about Christmas in a local paper. Heidi has been supporting herself with shlock jobs. Clerking at the 7-Eleven. She begins to think, How can I ever make a living at this when I can't even make a single sale?

Then her creative writing instructor points out how tough the short-story market is to crack. Why not try a novel?

Well, okay, why not?

The next two years are spent writing her novel, *Dreamtime.* She polishes and hones every word. Okay, it comes time to sell it. Heidi (by this time no longer a young writer) tries to get an agent. Ooooooooo, not so easy. Queries and sample chapters are sent out; more rejections come back. Some of them say nice things. *We like your style. Nice characterizations.*

After six months or a year of trying, an agent finally says he'll take *Dreamtime* on. In the meantime, Heidi has made a single sale to a not-too-bad literary magazine, so things are indeed looking up. And another story came in sixth in a contest. Sixth out of three hundred entries. The trouble is, the "sale" is paid in copies of the magazine and the contest only gives a certificate. Heidi has still not made a dime in her profession after seven years of working hard at it.

Dreamtime starts to make the rounds. Arbor House, Atheneum, Atlantic Monthly Press, Bantam Books. Some of the editors send along kind notes. *Great setting. Loved your use of language.* One or two even write detailed suggestions for revision. *Clear up some confusion in the dream sequences. Make the mother more sympathetic. Put the engagement scene earlier in the book.*

By this time Heidi is damn tired of clerking at 7-Eleven and driving a fifteen-year-old car. So she says to herself, I'd better get some training so I can get a real job and support my writing habit. Become a dental hygienist. Or maybe get a teaching job. Something that'll sustain me until I can get a novel published.

So a year is spent getting a teaching credential. And then not much writing gets done the first year of teaching because it's tough starting a new job. And she has a boyfriend now and they've been talking about getting married and, well, Heidi would like to be married . . .

So the once-young writer gets married and has a job and hasn't written anything in two years, and so the hell with it until maybe next summer. And then next summer there's a trip to take, there are books to be read, summer school to go to to sharpen one's teaching skills. There's a baby on the way.

So maybe next year, she tells herself. Maybe next year she'll get down to it. And soon Heidi is thinking of herself as someone who will someday be a writer. Maybe when she retires. She has, without really knowing it, broken faith with herself.

Once faith is broken, the writer is unlikely to go back to writing, ever.

Heidi was following the common path of most writers who eventually succeed. First the rejections, then the learning of craft, then more rejections, then personalized rejections, then small sales, and then the big one that makes you an overnight success. It's a long road for most writers, and many quit just as they complete the building of their launching pad, but before their rocket is launched.

There's another kind of losing faith, a very serious kind. It's often committed by the writer who can't quite find his way to the top of the mountain, a writer who has met with some success, but feels he or she hasn't yet made it. Maybe the writer has sold a few paperback originals. Or even a hardback that maybe got good reviews but only mediocre sales. If only there was some way to reach inside, this writer thinks, and pull out a little more talent, a little more something . . .

With each novel, as the writer finds himself not on the best seller list, he feels more and more frustrated. To relieve the terrible feeling of frustration, the writer might drink. Take a little speed. Cocaine. LSD.

Under the spell of the drug, the writer feels a sudden burst of optimism; the cloud of frustration dissipates. The writer believes he sees clearly for the first time in his life and plunges full speed ahead toward a new horizon.

Which, of course, is like a lemming heading for the sea.

Booze and drugs may be nice recreation, but the moment the writer looks to them for inspiration, he is lost. The writer loses faith with his own creativity and makes a deadly mistake, one that might finish him not only as a writer but as a human being.

So if drugs aren't the answer, what is the answer to discouragement?

Discouragement is generally a result of envying those who are more successful, or get more critical acclaim, or don't ever get rejected.

I have not gotten rich writing. Not yet, anyway, though I'm working on it. I'm not starving, but I'm not driving a Rolls either. I often have to turn to my Visa card for help between royalty checks. I've not found the mother lode in publishing, but I have had other rewards.

Frequently I go to a local college campus to do research in its fine library. The college is located on a high hill where on a clear day you can see most of the San Francisco Bay Area. You can see the freeways and the freight yards and the skyscrapers in San Francisco, and planes landing and taking off at three busy airports. You get a strong feeling of the hubbub of modern life, people hustling from place to place in pursuit of—what?

Stuff.

That's right, stuff. TVs and stereos and new cars and condos in the country. Stuff. The stuff you see advertised on TV. Toyotas and BMWs, stuff like that.

So when I sit in the library surrounded by books and look out on the hubbub I think, What is it that I'm in pursuit of? Art. I'm trying to write a damn good novel. One that is moving, dramatic, and says something important about the human condition. If in the pursuit of this I make a little money, so much the better. But if I don't? Well, I can do without the stuff. And I feel a little sorry for all those poor slobs down there pursuing stuff that just wears out and rusts and needs repainting.

Writing a damn good novel and getting it published gives me far more lasting pleasure than owning a Porsche turbo Carrera. A few good reviews, a few people saying, "I read your novel and was gripped beginning to end." That is more rewarding to me than a fistful of stock options.

Writing about writing has its rewards as well. Strangers come up to me and say they read *How to Write a Damn Good Novel* and they found it extremely helpful. Think of it, maybe long after I'm dead some kid in Nebraska will find a dusty copy of this book and it will help him, perhaps, to see that it is possible for him or her to become another Peter Benchley or Stephen King; a Jane Austen or Margaret Mitchell; a Stephen Crane or Fyodor Dostoevksy. Maybe even a Franz Kafka.

If I do become wildly successful down the line somewhere, you'll still be able to find me in the same college library surrounded by a stack of books, occasionally gazing out the window at the hubbub below, feeling sorry for those poor slobs pursuing their stuff.

6 . WRONG LIFESTYLE

After I gave a talk about the writer's life to a group of writers and aspiring writers, a smartly dressed woman in her early thirties came up to me and said that she had always wanted to be a writer. She said she had several good ideas for novels that she would love to write, but she had a problem and thought maybe I could give her some advice.

Every day she commuted an hour and a half to work and back, routinely worked nine- and ten-hour days, and did most of the housework. The only time she could get to her typewriter was on the weekends, and then her husband always wanted to go some-where because he, too, worked hard during the week.

I asked her whether she had any kids.

No, she didn't, she replied.

I suggested she quit her job.

She smiled sheepishly and said she couldn't do that. They had a big mortgage and her husband liked to travel, so they were making payments on a Winnebago. Her husband would kill her, she said, if she quit her job.

I said she should get another husband.

She blinked with astonishment. She said I was kidding, of course.

I was not kidding, I said. There are a lot of husbands out there—find one who will support your writing.

She walked away, muttering that I was a lunatic.

I may be, but that doesn't change the facts. You can't become a writer if you surround yourself with no-sayers. And if your spouse or live-in lover or roommate is not supporting you, you will have to change either their minds or your living arrangements.

Your ship won't make much headway dragging an anchor.

If you want to change the people you live with, you will prob-ably have to play what I call the writer's Big Scene. You bring your significant others together and tell them that you've made the de-cision to become a writer, a damn good one, and in order to become a damn good writer you will need their assistance and support. This means that you will be locked away in your cubbyhole, study, basement, back of the garage, or whatever for long hours at a time and you can't be disturbed. You will be going to writers' groups and taking classes, you'll be reading a lot more, and when the inevitable rejection letters come, you will need a good kick in the rump to get going again.

Playing the Big Scene impresses upon your significant others how important this is to you, how failure at this would be a terrible blow, and that they should keep their opinions of why you should not embark upon your career to themselves. You are going into this with total commitment and you're not interested in any gloom and doom predictions. And that's final.

Sometimes the Big Scene gets results, sometimes it doesn't. Sometimes it takes two or three Big Scenes for them to catch on to how serious you are.

Of course you will have to demonstrate your commitment by not allowing yourself to be distracted by a good program on television, neighbors who just stopped by, or a nice spring day calling you into the garden to plant tomatoes. The time you've scheduled for writing is for writing, and that's that.

I don't answer my telephone when I'm writing, I let my machine do it, even if it's my agent calling with good news. I don't answer my doorbell. If it's the Jehovah's Witnesses, they will just have to come by some other time to save my immortal soul. Right now I'm writing.

A writer must be prepared to say, "I can't talk right now, I'm writing," to his or her sister or brother or mother or father or kids. If they get miffed—well, they'll have to get over it. You have to impress upon people that when you're off in your cubbyhole you are gone. You aren't even on the planet and you can't be located.

You say you don't want to offend anyone? You say you couldn't be rude? You say you have to be available to your friends and loved ones when they need you? You say your sister is having marital problems and wants to cry on your shoulder? Your best friend needs help with his income tax? Your kids want you to show them how to tie fishing lures or bake cookies or hook up the VCR?

You cannot soar with the eagles if you're wasting your precious time gaggling with the geese. Do you want to be a writer or don't you? If you are going to be a writer, the only kind worth being is a damn good one, and the only way to be a damn good one is to, by God, give it everything you've got.

Giving it everything you've got means you will have to give it a lot of your time. To give it a lot of your time, you will have to *not* give a lot of your time to other things, like jobs, friends, family, and cleaning toilet bowls.

Giving time to one's profession makes perfect sense to people who want to become surgeons. A surgeon, during his or her training, is never home. A surgeon in training will often spend forty-eight or more hours straight at the hospital—attending classes, going on rounds, cutting open a lot of people and sewing them back up again.

An aspiring musician may practice ten or twelve hours a day for *years* before achieving a professional level of competency. An Olympic athlete, a ballet dancer, a stage magician all have to trade a huge slice of their time on earth for professional competency. Becoming a damn good novelist takes as much time, effort, and energy as becoming a damn good gymnast, a damn good figure skater, a damn good dentist, a damn good hired assassin, a damn good anything.

To become a damn good novelist you will have to put in your time writing. And that means that you won't be doing things other people do because you won't have time for them.

But what if you've got kids and responsibilities and the like? Okay, you will have to have a job, a secondary career, but it cannot be the center of your life. The writing will have to be the center of your life. Faulkner has been quoted as having said: "Everything goes by the board: honor, pride, decency . . . to get the book written. If a writer has to rob his mother, he will not hesitate; the *Ode on a Grecian Urn* is worth any number of old ladies."

I have personally witnessed hundreds of writers fail because they were not able to organize their lives around writing. The writing is put off and put off and put off.

Why is this?

Here's a guess: Writing is painful. Writing is hard work. Writing is sometimes a bitch. To be a damn good novelist you will have to write with pain, you will have to work hard, and you will have to do it despite the fact that it's a bitch.

And through it all you will have to grow. A regular program of growth should be included in any writer's lifestyle.

True, you will grow as a novelist if all you do is get older.

You will grow as a novelist if all you do is write.

But to become a damn good novelist, the best you can become, you'll have to do more than just live and write. You will have to study, too. You'll have to read and study the masters of your particular genre.

A novelist, of course, does not read novels just for enjoyment. A novelist reads with a writer's eye, looking at how these books are constructed, how the characters are motivated, how the conflicts develop, how the characters grow, how the climaxes come off. If novel writing is your game, you will study novels the way a student architect looks at buildings—not only at the veneer, but also at the beams and crossbeams, the plumbing, the wiring, and the foundation.

A damn good novelist in the making will study human beings and the minutiae of their lives: how they walk and talk, what they hope and dream, and what they sprinkle on their breakfast cereal. A novelist is a collector of tidbits that can be used later in the making up of characters. Some writers keep notebooks every day, jotting down every bit of detail they can about the people around them: their dress, their mannerisms, the way they shrug their shoulders, and the way their dandruff falls on their shoulders.

Another kind of study that ought to be integrated into a writer's everyday life is the study of craft. One of the great blessings of this profession is that it is forever opening itself up, an endless horizon of discovery. As you grow in your craft, through study you will find there is ever more to learn—about dramatic effects, about style, about word usage, and so on. There is no end to it. You can just keep learning for as long as you live, which is really wonderful.

7. FAILURE TO PRODUCE

Here's how a day's writing might go:

You plan to write, say, at ten in the morning. You make yourself some coffee first. While it's brewing you notice the newspaper beckoning you from the kitchen counter where your spouse left it. So you have to read all about the terrible earthquake in Tibet, the helicopter crash in Kenya, and "Dear Abby." Then a friend calls, wanting to chat. She's all broken up because her boy didn't get all *A*s in kindergarten. It's now ten forty-five. Got to get writing. But first, a second cup of coffee, finish the paper. Find out what's up with Doonesbury.

Eleven. Sit down at the ole word processor. Nothing seems right. Gotta adjust the blinds. Turn on some light rock on the radio. Stare at the screen. Too cool in the room. Go get a sweater, come back, sit down, stare at the screen. No bright ideas come to mind. Get up, get third cup of coffee. Clean up breakfast dishes. The cat wants out.

It's now eleven forty-five. Almost time for lunch. If you start now, you think, it'll be lunchtime just as you get rolling. Better start after lunch.

So you watch a "Leave It to Beaver" rerun.

After lunch you sit down again. Get some nice music going on the stereo. A full coffee cup. Get the blinds adjusted just right. Get on a lighter sweater. Reset the thermostat. Let the cat in. Then, just as you get going, the mail comes. How can you write with all those letters calling out to you to be freed from their envelope prisons? So to the rescue you go.

The bank has sent a check back. It irks you that they say you're overdrawn when you're not. You want to straighten it out right now, but damn it, it's time to write.

So you sit down to write. The checkbook calls to you from the other room. It must be balanced and balanced now. How can you write your novel with an unbalanced checkbook calling to you?

And so it goes.

If it isn't the checkbook, it's your looney brother, who wants to cry on your shoulder because he scratched the fender on his new Honda. Or the windows need washing, the floor needs cleaning, the lettuce for tonight's salad went limp.

Well, at some point you have to decide what you want out of life. Crisp lettuce, clean floors, a balanced checkbook, or a novel on the rack at the 7-Eleven store. If you have decided you want to be a novelist, the novel writing will have to come first; you won't be able to let the time slip away. When it's time to write, it's time to write.

What if the lawn needs cutting? You say, the lawn will have to wait. And the car won't get washed and the groceries won't get bought. The writing comes first.

Does that mean that you have to live in a pigpen and never play golf? Of course not.

But if you've decided you have fifteen hours a week in which to write, and you've set aside those fifteen hours, those are the hours you write and nothing short of a burning house or an emergency appendectomy should stop you from using those fifteen hours to write.

This kind of failure to produce is called *time slipping away.* Time can slip away in little slivers like the icicles you break off that form in your freezer, or it can slip away in huge chunks, like icebergs breaking off from a glacier.

There's another kind of failure to produce. It's called "writer's block."

In *How to Write a Damn Good Novel* I included a short discourse on writer's block in terms of fear of failure and fear of success. I now have a completely different view of it.

Writer's block, I believe, comes from a subconscious wish to be a martyr. Blocked writers are the Saint Sebastians of the writing profession.

What would you think if you heard this story:

> A bricklayer by the name of Big Jake Johnson goes to work one day. He works for High Rolling Builders and they're building a subdivision outside of Dallas. Big Jake is known as a real artist among bricklayers. Fancy fireplaces and patios a specialty. One bright, clear October day he shows up to work a little late. He'd stopped by the park, he says, to admire the pigeons. Nice colors in their necks.
>
> Anyway, his hod-carrier has mixed up the mortar and has lugged a pile of number four bricks up the hill to the back of a mansion High Rolling is building. Big Jake is supposed to lay down the brick walk going to the reflecting pool by the tennis court.
>
> So Big Jake has his cup of coffee and looks at the blueprints. A vague feeling of fear comes over him as his fingers trace the lines of the blueprints. He keeps staring at the blueprint, then at the pile of bricks, then at the mortar. Soon, drops of blood begin to form on his forehead.

He drops the blueprint and goes to the foreman, who sees him coming and already is nodding his head.

"Bricklayer's block, eh?"

Big Jake sadly nods his head. "I just can't do it today," he says. "Who knows, I may never be able to hold a trowel in my hand again."

The foreman lays a comforting hand on Big Jake's shoulder and tells him how sad it is.

Okay, so Big Jake goes home and drops on the couch. His wife, Orinda, says, "What's the matter, hon?"

"Bricklayer's block."

"What's that mean?"

"I just can't seem to do it today."

"Do we still get paid?"

"Well, no."

"How long is it going to last?"

"There's just no telling."

"Sounds like plain lazy to me."

"Hey, if writers can get writer's block, then I can get bricklayer's block."

Orinda goes into the kitchen, gets out a rolling pin, goes back in the living room and whacks Big Jake with it, right on the crown of the cranium, requiring thirty-four stitches.

And Big Jake never had bricklayer's block again.

If you've ever met someone "suffering" from writer's block, they will tell you all kinds of stories of how they sit and stare at blank paper or their computer screen and they just can't produce anything, no matter how much they try. If only they could, the implication is, they would produce masterpieces. But their genius will not let them proceed: They are stopped by their own human frailty, because nothing but the image of perfection that is in their mind would do (their standard being so much higher than that of us unblocked mortals who are writing crap), but it just refuses to gush out.

You see, of course, what writer's block is doing for them. It's allowing them to get sympathy for this terrible affliction and at the same time pass themselves off as a genius without ever having to submit anything to public scrutiny.

Don't let them get away with it.

Whenever I meet one of these tortured souls I tell them I have another way of spelling writer's block: C-H-I-C-K-E-N.

The blocked writer is not afraid of success or failure. What he or she is afraid of is that the writing will not stand up to the writer's own standard. Whose does?

To avoid such traps as time slippage and writer's block, look at writing the way a real bricklayer looks at his job. Writing is a job. It takes time and effort, the same as any other. Set yourself production goals. Three pages a day will get you a 270-page draft of a novel in three months.

The writing of a novel is a two-stage process. The first stage is to draft it; the second stage is to correct what you do in the first stage. Writing and rewriting. Draft it, then edit it.

A lot of so-called writer's block comes from a confusion of these two processes. Don't edit it until it's all written down. When you write a draft, don't look back. Turn off that editor up there in your brain.

Make the decision that you will never be caught in the trap of nonproduction. From now on, you will write, write, write, write, write, every day of the week and every week of the year.

And to do it well, you should write with passion. Which is the subject of the last chapter.

NINE

WRITING WITH PASSION

WHY NOW IS THE BEST
TIME IN HISTORY TO BE
A FICTION WRITER

Writers are in luck. This is the information age, and the writer's stock-in-trade is information. In the history of the world there has never been a better time to be a fiction writer than right now.

The invention of the word processor and high-speed quality printers is one reason. Editing, inserting, and moving text were nightmares when writers were writing on a clay tablet, or on paper with a quill pen, the fountain pen, the ballpoint pen, or a typewriter. Now it's just a matter of pushing a few fun buttons. In the olden days (just a few years ago), if you didn't like a paragraph in a finished draft there was no way to change it without retyping the entire manuscript. Now, zip-zip, zoom, bah, and there you are—rewritten and reprinted before you can say WordPerfect 3.1.

Another reason this is the best time in history to be a fiction writer is that more creative help is available than ever before. More than 600 colleges and universities in the United States offer creative writing classes. Private writers' self-help groups abound. Bookstores are packed with how-to-write books. Writers' conferences, seminars, and workshops are held in every part of the country.

Markets, too, are proliferating. Since Vintage Press with their

"Contemporaries" series started selling literary novels in trade paperback originals, imitators of their success have come onto the scene like the charge of the light brigade. Romance novels are a *billion*-dollar industry. The markets for mysteries, westerns, science fiction, fantasy, and young adults have never been better.

Small presses are spreading like crabgrass since the invention of cheap laser printers, which for $1,000 or $1,500 can for all practical purposes duplicate the work of a $20,000 typesetter. Self-publishing has passed from vanity to being a viable alternative—and potentially an extremely profitable one. I personally know of a poet who self-published a book of poems at a cost of $1.25 each and sold 18,000 copies at $9.95, at which point she sold the publishing rights to a New York house for $50,000.

We are living in an age of global economy, and opportunities for foreign sales abound. It's common for an American fiction writer now to make more money selling to, say, Great Britain, Europe, and Japan than in the United States.

In the forties and fifties there were perhaps 150 literary agents doing business in the United States. Now there are more than 900.

Novels are often optioned for motion pictures and television. Here, too, things have never been better. Cable TV movies, made-for-video cassette movies, and the Fox network—all hungry for good story material—have recently come onto the scene.

There has never been a better time in the history of the world to be a fiction writer. But people don't become fiction writers just because the window of opportunity is wide open.

There are other rewards. Rewards that transcend the possibilities of most other occupations. Where else can you have such a powerful effect on people's lives? Prisoners locked in the dankest dungeon might read your novel and find their escape or even deliverance. People in all walks of life might be transported from their daily drudgery. Schoolkids a hundred years from now might read what you've written and be moved by it.

In *The Art of Fiction* John Gardner says, "fiction provides, at its best, trustworthy but inexpressible models. We ingest metaphors of good, wordlessly learning to behave more like Levin than like Anna (in *Anna Karenina*), or more like the transformed Emma (in Jane Austen's novel) than like the Emma we first meet in the book. This subtle, for the most part wordless, knowledge is the 'truth' great fiction seeks out."

Gardner is 100 percent right. It is through stories that the values of our culture are transmitted to the young. How else do we learn what a hero is? What courage is? Honor? What it means to persevere in the face of great difficulties and terrors. How to love. How to relate to other human beings. The meaning of friendship. How to die with dignity.

The act of writing novels benefits the writer as well the reader. Novel writing teaches the writer a great deal about life. A good novelist must be a good observer, and as you train yourself in novel writing you will become an ever better observer. As you struggle with your characters, trying to understand them, motivate them, and make them real and believable with real guts and real guilts, you will find you are seeing the world with new eyes, and you will find within yourself new strength.

If you're around fiction writers much—despite their bloated egos and penchant for braggadocio—you will find them generally an extremely tolerant bunch. The reason is that they have vicariously experienced what it is like to be a member of a persecuted minority, say, or to suffer from extreme age, or to be infirm, or to be in wars and famines and family struggles, or in abusive relationships; as a result, fiction writers generally lack the prejudices found in the populace at large.

The act of writing fiction improves concentration. It improves mental acuity the way football practices improves a football player's performance. You will become a better reader as well as a better writer.

Writing novels may also give you the novelist's high.

Here's how the novelist gets the high: She sits down to write a scene. If she's wise, she's probably working from an outline. She knows, as an example, that the hero is supposed to ask the heroine's father for her hand in marriage. She might start the scene, sense it's going wrong, stop writing, erase or delete a sentence, then start again, sense it's wrong, stop, delete . . .

The writing is going badly. It's time for another cup of coffee. Settled in again in front of the keyboard, she stares at the wall, hums to herself, smokes a cig, sips coffee, and dreams . . .

Finally the scene starts to come clear in her mind. From someplace deep in her subconscious, it begins to float into her consciousness. She sees it happening on the viewing screen of her mind.

She starts to type, transcribing rather than creating the drama that the characters are acting out on their own like magic. As this happens, in the rush to get it down, the adrenaline pumping, she starts to feel exhilarated. Her heart beats faster, her blood pressure goes up, her fingers fly across the keys. It's like nothing else. It's like going to the moon on a motorcycle.

Usually, in an hour or two, the novelist is exhausted, but satisfied, and can relax, feeling tingly all over from the rush of excitement. This is the writer's high.

The writer's high is what reinforces this mysterious compulsion to write and rewards the creative act long before a check ever arrives from a publisher. The writer's high is such a powerful influence on some writers that nothing else matters—whether they publish or not becomes irrelevant. They've become writing junkies, hooked on the creative act.

There is no better way to spend your days on earth. But the biggest question is always: If I go for it, will I succeed? My answer is yes. And I guarantee it.

THE JAMES N. FREY
100 PERCENT GUARANTEE
OF SUCCESS

Anyone with a passionate desire will succeed if he gives himself to it fully, knuckles down and masters the craft, works hard, has good teachers and reliable readers, learns how to re-dream the dream and rewrite in answer to criticism, and actively pursues the selling of the script in a businesslike manner. I guarantee it 100 percent.

I know what you're thinking. You're thinking it can't be true. Not everyone can be a novelist. But I assure you, it is true. I *absolutely guarantee* it.

I can make that claim because I have a lot of experience in failing, trying again, failing, trying again—and finally succeeding.

Here's my story:

I always knew I was going to be a writer. And because I was born with the desire, I thought I was naturally born with the talent and didn't have to do anything special to prepare myself. I'd just knock off a novel in a few weeks, I thought, and fame and fortune—

my natural birthright—would come knocking at my door. Such was my attitude when I was in my early teens.

As a result of my firm belief in the fantasy of what a huge talent I was, I didn't study very hard. In fact, I had just about the worst grade point average in the history of my high school: 58 percent (or about a 1.0 in a 4-point system). My highest grade was an 82 in Driver's Ed. Naturally, colleges were not sending me offers of academic scholarships. When the time came, I didn't graduate with my class.

That really didn't bother me much. I landed a job as a soda jerk and took a couple of night school courses in English literature—hoping, I guess, to find out what my competitors like D. H. Lawrence and Herman Melville were up to. I paid little attention to the professors—I knew better than they did—and got *D*s, but I was not in the least discouraged. I was, of course, committing Fatal Mistake Number Six: living the wrong lifestyle. My father, seeing I was just a hopeless dreamer, was in despair. He thought my ambition to be a writer was a little nutty anyway. He wanted me to be a dentist or an insurance man. Or a banker, like him. Something with a future.

I moved from upstate New York to California to pursue my fantasy of writing a damn good novel, becoming famous, and retiring to my yacht before I was twenty-five.

Instead, I ended up being a machinist apprentice at the U.S. naval shipyard in Vallejo, California. I had to eat while awaiting fame and it was the only job I could get. Reality was beginning to make itself felt in my dim consciousness.

For my apprenticeship I was required to take a night school course in English at the local junior college. They gave me an entrance test, which qualified me for the lower-level bonehead course. I was outraged, of course. My fellow classmates were mostly recent Filipino immigrants whose native language was Tagalog. I quickly found out they knew more English grammar than I did. I decided I'd better buckle down and learn a little something. Since I was soon going to out-Hemingway Hemingway, it might help to know a little of the mechanics. Augment my genius.

During those years I didn't get much fiction writing done: Fatal Mistake Number Seven. In fact, by the time I was twenty-three I had yet to write anything. I was learning how to make submarines, play golf and poker, drink beer. I finally wrote a short story and submitted it to a new literary journal the junior college was putting out. They received six submissions and published five of them. That's right, mine was the reject.

I was crushed. The realization that I wasn't going to be the next Hemingway was finally beginning to dawn in my peanut. That was in 1965. I didn't write any fiction again until after I had finished my B.A. degree in 1969, when I started my first novel. I had come to a decision: Since the short story was obviously not my form, I was going to commit myself to becoming a novelist. Give it my all.

The first thing I did was try to get into a creative writing graduate program. I tried the big, more popular ones: Iowa, Irvine, San Francisco State, the University of California at Davis, and so on. Ten or twelve of them, and they all rejected me.

Sometimes these rejections hurt so much that I'd quit writing for a few days, a week, a month. I hadn't learned yet that rejections are just part of the game and so was committing Fatal Mistake Number Five: I wasn't keeping faith.

During the next few years I may not have made all the bad mistakes an apprentice novelist can make, but I made the big ones. Some were whoppers. I wrote the wrong kind of books. Serious, philosophical works, full of existential angst and leaden with symbols that symbolized I hadn't the foggiest idea what, which is Fatal Mistake Number Two: trying to be literary. When I got good criticism, I didn't attempt to re-dream the dream and rewrite: Fatal Mistake Number Four. In addition, I was guilty as well of ego-writing: Fatal Mistake Number Three.

Then I switched and tried stuff more suited to my abilities. I abandoned my first two novels because even I could see they weren't going anywhere. My third one, *The Deuce of Trump*, I completed and eventually submitted. It was rejected by an agent and an editor in the same week, so I put the book in a drawer and never sent it out again, without realizing they both were telling me it just needed a little more work—Fatal Mistake Number One again: being timid. My next effort, *The Cockroach*, was autobiographical, and because I hadn't resolved any of the issues I was exploring in the book in my own life, I could never resolve them in the story. Then I failed to finish four novels in a row because I lost faith in them. Fatal Mistake Number Five again.

Finally, I switched to thrillers and mysteries, but the mistakes multiplied.

I let an incompetent agent represent me, and even after it dawned on me he was a knucklehead, I stayed with him for two more years—because as long as I had an agent I felt like a writer. Besides, I didn't have the guts to dump him. Fatal Mistake Number One—timidity—again. Then I signed a multibook contract for pennies right after I sold my first novel, which wasted three potentially very productive years. I found teaching a nice diversion, so I let it gobble up all my time. Fatal Mistake Number Seven again.

When it comes to mistakes, I'm an expert.

I got lucky at times, too, such as when I met the right teacher, Lester Gorn, who is probably the greatest creative-writing teacher in the United States, and a world-class structuralist critic. He's been drumming the principles of the craft into my thick head now for over twenty years.

I got lucky, too, with my second agent, Susan Zeckendorf, who proved a great salesperson, who knows the business, is energetic, forthright, and who believes in me. She kept me from drowning more than once, and if I listened to her more often I'd probably have books stacked in the front window of every B. Dalton's from coast to coast.

Another lucky break came when a friend said I should go to the Squaw Valley Community of Writers, which was a truly spiritually transforming event in my life. I attended half a dozen times as a participant, and am now on the staff. It has been a mind-stretching experience and I am deeply indebted to the staff and the participants who have instructed and inspired me. At conferences such as Squaw Valley, writing is seen as an art form and the writer is seen as an artist, a seeker and interpreter of truth. At the Squaw Valley Writers' Conference I first heard that it is the job of the writer to create a masterpiece. Every year my batteries get recharged by just being around a couple hundred kindred souls, all trying to write damn good fiction.

The luckiest thing that ever happened to me was meeting, falling hopelessly in love with, and marrying my wife, Elizabeth. She is blessing number one in my life, and is the reason I've survived all those fatal mistakes.

To attempt to write a truly damn good novel is to try your damnedest to write a masterpiece.

Gerald Brace says in *The Stuff of Fiction* that creating a masterpiece is "a matter of basic courage" because "the predicament of modern man is the premise." It is the artist's business, Brace says, "to confront truth." That is the first step in creating a masterpiece.

Confronting truth is a very painful business. Most people spend years on a psychiatrist's couch before they begin. A novelist trying to create a masterpiece will have to begin on page one, chapter one.

People who become damn good novelists write with commitment and passion and tell the truth. They show human beings and human behavior for what they are. People who write damn good novels know who they are as writers and what they are trying to accomplish. They have a vision. They have a truth to tell and are on fire to tell it.

If a writer has no vision of his or her work, if all the writer wants is to publish and make money, the work will lack depth. It will be mere entertainment without the power to move the reader profoundly. There can be little lasting satisfaction to creating such hack work.

What kind of a vision could a fiction writer have?

Any fiction writer might have a vision of himself or herself as a moral philosopher or a social critic. Or a utopian. Or a satirist. Or a prophet.

A mystery writer might, as an example, envision herself as an entertainer, a puzzle maker, but someone who cares about justice and truth and the necessity for uncovering the evil that lurks in people's souls. Or she might passionately want to take the form of the mystery and push the limits of the conventions.

A literary writer might have a passion for the poetic possibilities in fiction or for exploring life's absurdities or the ambiguities of love. Or showing us the destructive nature of poverty or war or drug abuse.

A science fiction writer might envision himself or herself as a herald of the future, a seer showing the reader the implications of current events on the lives of our descendants, perhaps holding up a mirror of the future that reflects our present follies.

Writers of historicals or sagas often have a passion for revealing the past and showing how the past affects the present.

A romance writer might want to show that love is a healing power in the world and that true commitment to another is the path to happiness.

To find your own vision you need to look deeply within yourself and find out what you believe is important in life. If you could change people's minds about something, what would it be? What do you hate? What makes your blood boil? What do you love? Where do you stand? What would you be willing to die for? What can you bring to a work that shows the world in a unique light? What would be your gift to your fellow human beings?

Aleksandr Solzhenitsyn hated the totalitarian government in power in the Soviet Union. He attacked that government with every word he wrote. His works have a depth that can come only from feeling passionately about his material. His work earned him the Nobel Prize in 1970.

Harriet Beecher Stowe suffered the loss of a child to cholera, which brought home to her the suffering of slaves who were forcibly separated from their children. She wrote *Uncle Tom's Cabin* (1852) to make her readers feel the same. Harriet Beecher Stowe's book sold an astounding 300,000 copies and gave enormous impetus to the antislavery movement in the mid-nineteenth century.

Ernest Hemingway had a vision. He wanted to write clean, crisp, clear prose that would be, he said, like an iceberg, 90 percent beneath the surface. He became by far the most imitated writer of his time.

Raymond Chandler and Dashiell Hammett, among others, sought to make literature out of the detective novel and transformed the genre.

Jean Auel had, as John Gardner says, "an almost demonic compulsiveness" about prehistoric people. She delved deeply into the subject and novelized her research. At the time, it was widely thought that no one would be interested in reading about primitive peoples. But she had a passion, and now her books have sold millions.

Joseph Wambaugh cares about cops and how their jobs grind them down. His passion and commitment come through every line.

Once you read one of his books, you'll never see cops the same way again.

Peter Benchley had always had a fascination with sharks. He read everything he could about them and wanted to create a powerfully suspenseful story that would not only grip the reader, but open people up to a subject he loved.

Stephen King has become the king of horror novels, but when he wrote *Carrie,* he was just starting out. He has shown us, in a most entertaining way, what happens when you mess with a telekinetic like Carrie. But more than that, his story is about the cruelty of unthinking teenagers and the psychological damage they can inflict on their peers, a subject he felt most strongly about.

Margaret Mitchell, the daughter of the president of the Georgia Historical Society, felt passionately that the nation needed to know of the antebellum South and how the American Civil War destroyed that way of life. Not only one of the great best sellers of all time, *Gone with the Wind* won the National Book Award and the Pulitzer Prize.

Fyodor Dostoyevsky was passionately interested in the idea of spiritual regeneration through suffering, which is the core of *Crime and Punishment.*

Jane Austen worked, in her words, "on a little bit of ivory with a very fine brush." Her passion was poking fun at the middle-class, provincial society that surrounded her.

Franz Kafka is a towering figure in twentieth-century literature. He lived in Central Europe and saw his world turned upside down by such titanic events as the First World War and the Russian Revolution. Modernism was being born, and men such as Freud and Jung and Einstein were turning the old world on its ear. He saw life as chaotic and absurd and man as a confused, alienated, isolated creature, and he wanted his reader to see them this way, too. This was his passion, and his works are now considered classics.

Stephen Crane's works, such as *The Red Badge of Courage,* are also classics. Stephen Crane helped found the American realism tradition, which includes Dreiser, Norris, Hemingway, Steinbeck, and many others. Stephen Crane thought of *The Red Badge of Courage* as a study of psychological fear rather than of heroism in war, as the previous writers on the subject had done.

Words are guns. If you feel strongly about something, aim your guns and fire. That's what having a vision means. Writing with a vision means you are writing with *"an almost demonic compulsiveness."*

If instead you create derivative work in imitation of others, if you create exploitive and sensationalistic work, you will not find much satisfaction. Only work you're committed to, that is deeply meaningful to you and your readers, gives any lasting satisfaction. You can write such work only if you envision yourself as a writer and know what you have to say to the world that is uniquely yours.

Melba Beals, who took a few of my workshops at U.C. Berkeley Extension, felt passionately about telling her story. She was one of the black children who had integrated all-white Central High in Little Rock in 1957. She wrote *Warriors Don't Cry,* an account of her experiences of being spit on and insulted, threatened, bullied, and terrorized. The book received a large advance from Pocket Books. It's an important book of lasting value because it was written with great passion and great heart.

Arnaldo Hernandez, who was a close friend and briefly a student of mine, was originally from Cuba. As a teenager he'd fought against Batista, but after Castro took over, he felt the fight for freedom had been betrayed. He published three damn good thrillers about spies fighting against the spread of communism.

Grant Michaels took a couple of my workshops. He has a passion to show gay people as real people, with all the same quirks and foibles, searching to end their loneliness and find meaningful relationships, just like everyone else. He sold a wonderful, wacky, comic mystery series to St. Martin's Press that does just that. His hero, Stani, is a gay hairdresser.

Another member of one of my workshops, Paul Clayton, felt strongly that the indigenous people of America got a raw deal at the hands of the Spanish, and he wrote a damn good historical novel about it called *Cacique.* It sold to Berkley Books. His advance was not large, but the editors want to see a sequel, so he has a good start on making a career.

Phyllis Burke, whom I was lucky enough to have in a couple of my workshops, was always fascinated by the way the public sees the famous, particularly JFK and Marilyn Monroe. She wrote a damn good, even brilliant, satirical novel about it called *Atomic Candy,* which was published by Atlantic Monthly Press and was widely reviewed and praised.

Another student of mine, April Sinclair, grew up on Chicago's south side during the height of the Civil Rights and Black Power movements. She longed to tell that story, to make her readers understand what it was like, she says, "to be black and female before and after black was considered beautiful." She worked damn hard for several years, writing and rewriting and honing her story and her prose to a high level of art and social commentary. Hyperion bought *Coffee Will Make You Black* the third day it was offered.

When you sit down to create a novel, mediate on what you want to say. Ask yourself what you feel strongly about. Ask yourself: What am I about as a writer? What is my mission? Where am I going? What do I stand for? What do I want my readers to say about me? What am I trying to achieve? What are my themes? A novel may explore one theme, or two, or even more.

"A writer," Gerald Brace says in *The Stuff of Fiction*, "must have something to say." By which he means, a writer must have something important to say. What do you have that is important to say?

To have something important to say does not mean that you want to preach. As Percy Marks warns in *The Craft of Writing* (1932), by writing from moral indignation the author "may write a sermon instead of a novel, and we do not read novels for preachments."

It helps to write a statement of your purpose, to get down on paper what you're trying to achieve as a writer as your life's work, and what you're trying to achieve in the particular book you're writing. It's a good idea to take a look at your statement once in a while and think about it. What do you really want to accomplish?

A friend of mine writes popular fiction. He writes about people who have committed great sins and feel that redemption is not possible. He writes about how big institutions—the justice system, spy agencies, large corporations—grind people up. He hopes his readers will be horrified and see things in a new light.

Another writer friend is a Buddhist who believes strongly in the power of compassion as a force for good in the world. Her characters, through intense inner agonies, always come to some kind of enlightenment, an enlightenment she hopes the reader shares.

Another friend writes romances. She hopes that her readers may be inspired by her plucky characters to take risks with their lives, to try new things, to experiment. Her aim is not to write great literature, but to write great romances, ones that show the healing power of love and what true commitment means.

The notion that a story has a premise goes beyond its technical aspects, which were discussed in Chapters Four and Five. When you write a story you are saying, Here, reader, take a look. Given these characters and this situation, human nature is such that it will end up this way. This is your truth. This is what you must feel strongly about if you are going to write a damn good novel.

Writing is an act of sharing experience. It is a ritual of transformation. There is no such thing as "just an entertainment." What you're writing has an emotional and spiritual effect on readers, and if you do your job well, the effect will be profound.

When you're writing fiction, you have the possibility of doing good in the world, of making a difference, of changing people's lives. To do so, you must reach deep inside yourself and tap the root of your passions; that is where you'll find your power. Once you find it, you've opened the gateway to the possibility of writing a damn good novel, perhaps even a masterpiece, a novel that will profoundly affect readers well into the next century and even beyond.

BIBLIOGRAPHY

Aristotle. "The Poetics" in *The Basic Works of Aristotle*. Edited by Richard McKeon. New York: Random House, 1941.

Austen, Jane. *Pride and Prejudice*. New York: Washington Square Press, 1960.

Benchley, Peter. *Jaws*. New York: Doubleday and Company, Inc., 1974.

Brace, Gerald Warner. *The Stuff of Fiction*. New York: W. W. Norton and Company, 1969.

Camus, Albert. *The Stranger*. New York: Alfred A. Knopf, Inc., 1946.

Clayton, Hamilton. *The Art of Fiction*. New York: The Odyssey Press, 1939.

Crane, Stephen. *The Red Badge of Courage*. New York: The New American Library, 1960.

DeVoto, Bernard. *The World of Fiction*. Boston: The Writer, Inc., 1956.

Dostoevsky, Fyodor. *Crime and Punishment*. New York: The Literary Guild of America, Inc., 1953.

Egri, Lajos. *The Art of Dramatic Writing*. New York: Simon and Schuster, 1946.

———. *The Art of Creative Writing*. New York: The Citadel Press, 1965.

Foster-Harris, William. *The Basic Formulas of Fiction*. Norman: University of Oklahoma Press, 1944.

———. *The Basic Patterns of Plot.* Norman: University of Oklahoma Press, 1959.

Fowles, John. *The French Lieutenant's Woman.* Boston: Little, Brown & Co., 1969.

Gardner, John. *On Becoming a Novelist.* New York: Harper & Row Publishers, 1983.

———. *The Art of Fiction: Notes on Craft for Young Writers.* New York: Alfred A. Knopf, 1984.

Hall, Oakley. *The Art & Craft of Novel Writing.* Cincinnati: Writer's Digest Book, 1989.

Hugo, Victor. *Les Misérables.* Translated by Norman Denny. New York: Penguin Books, 1980.

Kafka, Franz. *The Trial.* Translated by Willa and Edwin Muir. New York: Alfred A. Knopf, Inc., 1937.

Kazantzakis, Nikos. *Zorba the Greek.* New York: Simon and Schuster, 1953.

Kesey, Ken. *Sailor Song.* New York: The Penguin Group, 1992.

King, Stephen. *Carrie.* New York: Doubleday and Company, Inc., 1974.

Knott, William C. *The Craft of Fiction.* Reston: Reston Publishing Co., 1977.

Koontz, Dean R. *How to Write Best-Selling Fiction.* Cincinnati: Writer's Digest Books, 1981.

Leonard, Elmore. *Maximum Bob.* New York: Delacorte Press, 1991.

Marks, Percy. *The Craft of Writing.* New York: Grosset and Dunlap, 1932.

Macauley, Robie and George Lanning. *Technique in Fiction.* Second Edition: Revised and Updated for a New Generation. New York: St. Martin's Press, 1987.

MacGowan, Kenneth. *A Primer of Playmaking.* New York: Random House, 1951.

Mitchell, Margaret. *Gone with the Wind.* New York: The MacMillan Company, 1936.

Peeples, Edwin A. *A Professional Storywriter's Handbook.* Garden City: Doubleday & Company, Inc., 1960.

Puzo, Mario. *The Godfather.* New York: G. P. Putnam's Sons, 1969.

Surmelian, Leon. *Technique of Fiction Writing: Measure and Madness.* Garden City: Anchor Books/Doubleday & Company, Inc., 1969.

Vonnegut, Kurt, Jr. *Breakfast of Champions.* New York: Delacorte Press, 1973.

Whitney, Phyllis A. *Guide to Fiction Writing.* Boston: The Writer, Inc., 1982.

Wolfe, Tom. *The Bonfire of the Vanities.* New York: Farrar, Straus, Giroux, 1987.

INDEX

African Queen, The (film), 77
agents (literary), 138, 143
Anna Karenina (Tolstoy), 38, 72, 138
Aristotle, 37
Art of Creative Writing, The (Egri), 1
Art of Dramatic Writing, The (Egri), 1, 51
Art of Fiction, The (Clayton), 35
Art of Fiction, The (Gardner), 6, 7, 54, 138–139
As I Lay Dying (Faulkner), 39
Atlantic, The, 124
Atomic Candy (Burke), 147
Auel, Jean, 145
Austen, Jane, 127, 138
  dual characters and, 43
  and the lit fuse, 31
  and the narrative voice, 85, 106
  and reader identification, 10
  and reader sympathy, 9
  and the reader's contract, 106
  and ruling passion, 42
  social disapproval and menace, 27
  story question, starting with, 24
  vision of, 146
  wacky characters and, 39

authenticity, 36–37
author as commentator, 86–87
author/reader contract, 99–109
  beyond the conventions, 103–106
  genre, 100–101
  literary, 102–103, 117–119, 142, 144
  mainstream, 101–102
  playing fair, 108–109
  unreliable narrator, 107–108

Barker, Clive, 86
Basic Formulas of Fiction, The (Foster-Harris), 1, 21
Baum, Frank L., 40
Beals, Melba, 147
Benchley, Peter, 127
  characters, competence of, 37
  characters/setting contrast, 40
  and the lit fuse, 31
  and reader empathy, 15–16
  and reader identification, 10
  and reader sympathy, 8
  social disapproval and menace, 27
  story question, starting with, 24
  vision of, 146
  and wacky characters, 39

Berne, Eric, 43
Bickman, Jack M., 1
blocked writers, 134–136
Bonfire of the Vanities, The (Wolfe),
    85
Brace, Gerald, 51, 144, 148
Breakfast of Champions (Vonnegut),
    86
Brontë, Emily, 39
Burke, Phyllis, 147

Cacique (Clayton), 147
California Writers Club, 120–121
Camus, Albert, 88–89
Captains Courageous (Kipling), 40
Carrie (King)
    characters, competence of, 37
    characters/setting contrast, 41
    dual characters and, 43
    and the lit fuse, 31
    narrative voice, 83, 89–90, 92–93,
        105–106
    reader empathy and, 14
    reader identification and, 10
    reader sympathy and, 9
    reader, transportation of, 17–18
    and the reader's contract, 105–106
    ruling passion and, 42
    social disapproval and menace, 27
    story question, starting with, 25
    vision of, 146
    wacky characters and, 39
Cervantes Saavedra, Miguel de, 38
chain reaction premise, 59–60
Chandler, Raymond, 145
Chaplin, Charlie, 39
chapter size, 104–105
characters
    and competence, 37
    contrasting with setting, 40–41
    dual, 43–47
    empathy with, 12–16
    identification with, 10–12
    and research, 36–37
    ruling passions, 41–43

    sympathy for, 8–10
    wacky, 38–40
    as wimps, 33–35
    worth knowing, 35–37
Clancy, Tom, 102
Clayton, Hamilton, 35
Clayton, Paul, 147
Cockroach, The (Frey), 52, 119, 142
Coffee Will Make You Black
    (Sinclair), 148
colloquial terms, 94
comic contrasted with tragic, 39
communication
    and fiction writing, xi
competence and character, 37
complications, development of, 58–
    59, 64, 65–66, 69–71
concept, 50–61. *See also* premise
*Connecticut Yankee in King Arthur's
    Court, A* (Twain), 40
"Contemporaries" series (Vintage
    Press), 137–138
contrast
    characters and setting, 40–41
    comic with tragic, 39
conventions, beyond the, 103–106
Craft of Fiction, The (Knott), 1, 87
Craft of Writing, The (Marks), 148
Crane, Stephen, 127
    characters/setting contrast, 40
    and the lit fuse, 31
    and the narrative voice, 106
    and reader empathy, 14–15
    and reader identification, 10
    and reader sympathy, 9
    reader, transportation of, 18–19
    and the reader's contract, 106
    and ruling passion, 42
    social disapproval and menace, 27
    story question, starting with, 25
    vision of, 146
Crime and Punishment (Dostoevsky)
    American version, 68–72
    characters/setting contrast, 40
    multipremise, 72

narrative voice, 83–85
reader identification and, 10
reader sympathy and, 9
reader, transportation of, 19–20
ruling passion and, 42
social disapproval and menace, 27
story question, starting with, 25
vision of, 146
critiques, 112–113

Dale Carnegie, 117
Day of the Jackal, The (Forsyth), 30
De Nero, Robert, 8
Defoe, Daniel, 8, 38
Deuce of Trump, The (Frey), 142
devices
chapter size, 104–105
journal and diary, 104
unreliable narrator, 107–108
DeVoto, Bernard, 6, 50, 51
Dickens, Charles, 8
Don Quixote (Cervantes Saavedra), 38
Dostoevsky, Fyodor, 127
characters/setting contrast, 40
and multipremise, 72
and the narrative voice, 83–85
and reader identification, 10
and reader sympathy, 9
reader, transportation of, 19–20
and ruling passion, 42
social disapproval and menace, 27
story question, starting with, 25
vision of, 146
Doyle, Sir Arthur Conan, 104
dream, failure to re-dream the, 121–123
dual characters, 43–47
Frankenstein, 43
Jekyll and Hyde, 43
Long John Silver, 43

ego-writing, 119–121, 142
Egri, Lajos, 1, 35, 51
Eliot, T. S., 119

empathy, 12–16
Eye of the Needle, The (Follett), 30

fabulists (South American), 103
faith, keeping the, 124–128, 142
Falstaff, 39
fatal mistakes (seven deadly)
being literary, 117–119, 142
ego-writing, 119–121, 142
failure to produce, 131–135, 141, 143
keeping the faith, 124–128, 142
lifestyle, 128–131, 141
re-dreaming the dream, 121–123
timidity, 111–117, 143
Farewell to Arms, A (Hemingway), 114
Fast, Howard, 102
Faulkner, William, 39, 107
fictive dream, 6–7
first vs third person, 87–93
Fleming, Ian, 101
Follett, Ken, 30
For Whom the Bell Tolls? (Hemingway), 114
Forsyth, Frederick, 30
Foster-Harris, William, 1, 21
Fowles, John, 87
French Lieutenant's Woman, The (Fowles), 87
Frey, Elizabeth, 143
Frey, James N., 1, 3, 36, 41, 49, 83, 127, 133, 140–143

Games People Play (Berne), 43
Gardner, John, 6, 7, 54, 138–139, 145
genre fiction, 100–101
mystery, 101, 144
romance, 100, 145
science, 101, 144–145
spy thrillers, 100
Godfather, The (Puzo), 11–12
Gone with the Wind (Mitchell)
characters, competence of, 37
characters/setting contrast, 40

Gone with the Wind (*continued*)
  and the lit fuse, 31
  multipremise, 72
  narrative voice, 82–83
  reader identification and, 10
  reader sympathy and, 9
  reader's contract, 106
  ruling passion and, 42
  social disapproval and menace, 27
  story question, starting with, 25
  vision of, 146
Gorn, Lester, *xi*, 50, 143
Grafton, Sue, 102

Hammett, Dashiell, 145
Hemingway, Ernest, 114, 145
Henry IV Part One and *Part Two*
  (Shakespeare), 39
Hernandez, Arnaldo, 147
historical novels, 102, 145, 147
Hitchcock, Alfred, 114
Homer, 37
honesty and writing, *xi*
horror fiction, 101
How to Write a Damn Good Novel
  I (Frey), 1, 3, 36, 41, 49, 83, 127,
  133
How to Write Best-Selling Fiction
  (Koontz), 29, 54
how-to-write books, 137
Hugo, Victor, 8, 24

identification with character, 10–12

jargon, 94
Jaws (Benchley)
  characters, competence of, 37
  characters/setting contrast, 40
  and the lit fuse, 31
  reader empathy and, 15–16
  reader identification and, 10
  reader sympathy and, 8
  social disapproval and menace,
  27
  story question, starting with, 24

  vision of, 146
  wacky characters and, 39
Joyce, James, 118

Kafka, Franz, 127
  characters/setting contrast, 40
  narrative voice, 106
  and reader empathy, 16
  and reader identification, 10
  and reader sympathy, 9
  reader, transportation of, 18
  and the reader's contract, 106
  social disapproval as menace, 27
  story question, starting with, 24
  vision of, 146
Kazantzakis, Nikos, 38–39
keeping the faith, 124–128, 142
Kesey, Ken, 28, 40, 91
King, Stephen, 9, 114, 127
  characters, competence of, 37
  characters/setting contrast, 41
  and dual characters, 43
  and the lit fuse, 31
  and the narrative voice, 83, 89–90,
  92–93, 105–106
  and reader identification, 10
  and reader empathy, 14
  and reader sympathy, 9
  reader, transportation of, 17–18
  and ruling passion, 42
  social disapproval and menace,
  27
  story question, starting with, 25
  vision of, 146
  and wacky characters, 39
Kipling, Rudyard, 40
Knott, Raymond C., 1, 87
Koontz, Dean, 29, 54, 102

Lawrence, D. H., 141
le Carré, John, 30, 101
Leigh, Janet, 114
Leonard, Elmore, 37, 90–91
lifestyle as a writer's problem, 128–
  131, 141

literary, danger of being, 117–119, 142
literary agents, 138, 143
literary fiction, 102–103, 144

mainstream fiction, 101–102
Marks, Percy, 148
Maximum Bob (Leonard), 90–91
Melville, Herman, 7, 38, 141
metafiction, 103
Michaels, Grant, 147
Mirrielees, Edith, 51
Misérables, Les (Hugo), 8, 24
mistakes (seven deadly)
    being literary, 117–119
    ego-writing, 119–121, 142
    failure to produce, 131–135, 141, 143
    keeping the faith, 124–128
    lifestyle, 128–131, 141
    re-dreaming the dream, 121–123
    timidity, 111–117, 143
Mitchell, Margaret, 127
    characters, competence of, 37
    characters/setting contrast, 40
    and the lit fuse, 31
    and multipremise, 72
    and the narrative voice, 82–83, 106
    and reader identification, 10
    and reader sympathy, 9
    and the reader's contract, 106
    and ruling passion, 42
    social disapproval and menace, 27
    story question, starting with, 25
    vision of, 146
Moby Dick (Melville), 7, 38
Moll Flanders (Defoe), 8, 38
moral and premise, 53–54
Mugaby, Sir Wilbur, 5
mystery fiction, 101, 144
Mystery Scene (magazine), 101
Mystery Writers of America, 101

narrator. *See* voice
New York Review of Books, 103

New York Times Book Review, 103
New Yorker, The, 124

Odyssey (Homer), 37
Oliver Twist (Dickens), 8
One Flew Over the Cuckoo's Nest (Kesey)
    character contrast and setting, 40
    menace and, 28
    opposing forces premise, 60–61
Owen, Jean Z., 1

Parker, Robert B., 102
Peeples, Edwin A., 34, 35, 39, 111
philosophical novels, 103, 144
Poetics (Aristotle), 37
premise, 50–61, 63–78
    changing, 63–67
    and complications, 58–59, 64, 65–66, 69–71
    examples, 55–61
    finding a, 51–53, 67–72
    moral, 53–54
    terms, 53–55
    theme, 54–55
premise, types of
    chain reaction, 59–60
    opposing forces, 60–61
    situational, 61
Pride and Prejudice (Austen)
    dual characters and, 43
    and the lit fuse, 31
    narrative voice, 85, 106
    reader identification and, 10
    reader sympathy and, 9
    and the reader's contract, 106
    ruling passion and, 42
    social disapproval and menace, 27
    story question, starting with, 24
    vision of, 146
    wacky characters and, 39
produce, failure to, 131–135, 141, 143
Professional Fiction Writing (Owen), 1

*Professional Storywriter's Handbook,
A* (Peeples), 34, 35, 39, 111
pseudo-rules, 2–3
  first vs third person, 87–93
  story question, starting with, 25
public speaking courses, 117
Publishers Weekly, 116
Puzo, Mario, 11–12

Raging Bull (film), 8
readers
  expectations of, 6
  transporting, 16–20
  See also author/reader contract
Red Badge of Courage, The (Crane)
  characters/setting contrast, 40
  and the lit fuse, 31
  narrative voice, 106
  reader empathy and, 14–15
  reader identification and, 10
  reader sympathy and, 9
  reader, transportation of, 18–19
  and the reader's contract, 106
  ruling passion and, 42
  social disapproval and menace, 27
  story question, starting with, 25
  vision of, 146
rejection, dealing with, 142
rejection forms, 124–125
research and characters, 36–37
romance fiction, 100, 145
Romance Writers of America, 101
ruling passions, 41–43

sagas, 102, 145
Sailor's Song (Kesey), 91
Samson and Delilah, 57–59
science fiction, 101, 144–145
self-publishing, 138
setting contrasted with characters,
  40–41
sex scenes, writing, 114–115
Shakespeare, William, 39
Shirley Valentine (Russell), 34
showing, not telling, 7

Sinclair, April, 147–148
situational premise, 61
Solzhenitsyn, Aleksandr, 145
small presses, 138
Sound and the Fury, The (Faulkner),
  107
South American fabulists, 103
spy thrillers, 100
*Spy Who Came in from the Cold,
  The* (le Carré), 30
Squaw Valley Community of
  Writers, 143
Squaw Valley Writer's Conference,
  143
Steele, Danielle, 102
Stevenson, Robert Louis, 8
Stowe, Harriet Beecher, 145
Stranger, The (Camus), 88–89
stream-of-consciousness, 103
Stuff of Fiction, The (Brace), 51, 144,
  148
suspense
  as curiosity, 21–25
  definitions of, 21, 25–26
  lighting the fuse, 29–31
  as menace, 25–29
Swanee Review, The, 124
sympathy, 7, 8–10

Tan, Amy, 37, 102
Technique in Fiction (Macauley/
  Lanning), 23, 83, 86, 103
theme and premise, 54–55
Three Faces of Eve, The (film), 46
timidity as a problem, 111–117, 143
Tolstoy, Leo, 38, 72, 138
tragic contrasted with comic, 39
transported readers, 16–20
Treasure Island (Stevenson), 8
Trial (Kafka)
  characters/setting contrast, 40
  narrative voice, 106
  reader empathy and, 16
  reader identification and, 10
  reader sympathy and, 9

Trial (Kafka) (*continued*)
  reader, transportation of, 18
  and the reader's contract, 106
  social disapproval as menace, 27
  story question, starting with, 24
  vision of, 146
truth and writing, *xi*, 138
Twain, Mark, 40

Uncle Tom's Cabin (Stowe), 145

Vintage Press, 137–138
vision, finding your own, 145
voice, 79–97
  author as commentator, 86–87
  changing, 104–105
  developing your own, 93–97
  first vs third person, 87–93
  personality of, 79–80
  strong narrative, 81–86
  tone, 95–97
  unreliable narrator, 107–108
Vonnegut, Kurt, Jr., 86

wacky characters, 38–40
  Hercule Poirot, 38

Nero Wolf, 38
Sherlock Holmes, 38, 104
Zorba the Greek, 38–39
Wambaugh, Joseph, 37, 145–146
War and Peace (Tolstoy), 38, 72
Warriors Don't Cry (Beals), 147
Weaveworld (Barker), 86
western fiction, 101
wimps as characters, 33–35
Wizard of Oz, The (Baum), 40
Wolfe, Tom, 85
women's fiction, 102
Woolf, Virginia, 118
World of Fiction, The (DeVoto), 6,
  50, 51
writer's block, 134–136
writer's conferences, 137, 143
Writer's Digest, 1
writer's self-help groups, 137
Writing Novels That Sell (Bickman),
  1
Wuthering Heights (Brontë), 39

Zeckendorf, Susan, 143
Zorba the Greek (Kazantzakis), 38–
  39